THE GREAT AMERICAN RASCAL

The Turbulent Life of Aaron Burr

Noel B. Gerson

SAPERE
BOOKS

THE GREAT
AMERICAN RASCAL

Published by Sapere Books.

20 Windermere Drive, Leeds, England, LS17 7UZ,
United Kingdom

saperebooks.com

ISBN: 978-1-80055-095-7.

Table of Contents

I live my life as I deem appropriate and fitting. I offer no apologies, no explanations — I hate them.

— AARON BURR

Chapter 1

Aaron Burr was his own worst enemy. A man of genius and charm, he could have been one of the greatest of Americans in an age of giants, but the defects in his personality led him down a self-destructive path, and like the protagonist in an ancient Greek tragedy, he alone was responsible for his ultimate doom.

Burr possessed every quality necessary for enduring success except one: He lacked a stability of character to match his gifts, which included a quick-witted, towering intellect, the zeal of a visionary, abundant physical courage, and an ability to inspire others. His own ambition destroyed him, and instead of assuming a place in the front rank of the founding fathers of the United States of America, he became the nation's first full-fledged villain.

No man ever lost the Presidency of his country by a narrower margin, and that prize would surely have been his in due time had he conducted himself differently. However, his yearning for glory made it impossible for him to wait, and he alienated all but a handful of his intimates. His rise to a place near the summit was swift, yet his decline was even more rapid, and he earned the contempt of men of integrity everywhere.

In spite of his misfortunes, however, Burr was always true to himself. It was this consistency that enabled him to maintain a curious dignity, even in the days when tragedy plagued him, and in the end he earned a measure of respect from his fellow citizens, although few admired him and few still were willing to accept his leadership.

The secret of his inner stature was his refusal to feel sorry for himself, and even his detractors have been forced to accord him a grudging salute for his stubborn tenacity in the face of adversities that would have overwhelmed a lesser man. The product of his times, he was also the victim of his era, and although it serves no useful purpose to speculate on his fate had he lived in another period, it is difficult to erase the haunting suspicion that he might well have realized the satisfaction of all his desires.

No eighteenth-century American boasted a more distinguished ancestry than Aaron Burr. His father, also named Aaron Burr, was an American-born Presbyterian clergyman and educator who could trace his lineage through hundreds of years of English history, earlier Burrs having gained prominence in government and politics. Rev. Burr was an honor graduate of Yale College and by the middle of the eighteenth century had become the second president of the College of New Jersey, later to change its name to Princeton. His wife, Esther, many years his junior, was the third daughter of Jonathan Edwards, the Massachusetts clergyman who was regarded as the major spokesman for the Puritan point of view in the Colonies.

They were married for almost four years before their son, whom they named Aaron, was born at Newark on February 6, 1756. They had one older child, a daughter named Sarah, who would remain close to her brother all of her life. In that same year a fever carried away Rev. Burr and his wife, and the orphaned children were taken to Massachusetts by their maternal grandfather. Esther Burr's brother, Timothy Edwards, made the youngsters his legal wards, and they grew up in his Elizabethtown home.

The Edwards family lived in comfortable circumstances, although they were not considered wealthy, and neither Aaron nor his sister, known in the family as Sally, were ever subject to any privations. Aaron was a small child, but his precocity more than compensated for his lack of physical stature. He was able to read at the age of four, and by five he could write; he was also fond of outdoor activities, and a handyman taught him to shoot, so that by the age of seven he was already familiar with pistols and muskets.

Uncle Timothy may have regretted his generosity many times. Young Aaron was a genius, it was true, but he was also an arrogant, unruly child who refused to accept discipline. On only one occasion was he given the rod, commonly used at that period to improve the conduct of small boys. Aaron was only six at the time, but he reacted with such blazing hatred that he was never whipped again. Edwards and his wife were unable to lose sight of the fact that the Burr children were not their own and consequently treated them with such lenience that Sally did not exaggerate, years later, when she said, "We were spoiled."

Young Aaron advanced so rapidly in Elizabethtown's one school that the two teachers were forced to admit their inability to handle him after he had been their pupil for a scant six months. Timothy Edwards decided to tutor the boy at home, but he could not devote as much time to the effort as was necessary. Accordingly, when Aaron was seven, a tutor named Tapping Reeve was hired. The association of teacher and student was destined to last for the rest of their lives, since Reeve, who became the founder of the Litchfield Law School, eventually married Sally Burr, thus becoming Aaron's brother-in-law.

A deep-seated ambition to advance as far and as rapidly as possible became evident in young Aaron from earliest childhood. He was always the leader in his associations with other boys, even though he was smaller than most of his contemporaries, but games quickly bored him, and he sought other distractions from the reading that consumed him for hours every day. He badgered Reeve into teaching him the rudiments of fencing and became such an accomplished swordsman that he won every match from his tutor. He also acquired a pair of dueling pistols and practiced his marksmanship on targets he set up in the Edwards yard.

By the time he was eleven Burr decided he was ready to attend college. He submitted an application to his father's school, the College of New Jersey, and his uncle took him to Princeton for a visit. The college authorities were dismayed: He was so short and slender he looked like a child of seven or eight. Accordingly, he was told he had failed to pass the entrance examinations and must, therefore, wait for at least two more years.

Burr was furious, believing the school had discriminated against him, and was particularly angry because his sense of competition demanded that he beat the record set by his grandfather, Jonathan Edwards, who had entered college at thirteen. He had no choice, however, as it did not occur to him to apply to any other school, his own code of loyalty demanding that he attend no college other than the one where his father had made a major contribution to higher education.

On his thirteenth birthday he again applied to the College of New Jersey, making a second visit there with his uncle. He achieved such high grades in the entrance examinations that he demanded admission to the junior class, which would have made it possible for him to obtain a degree in accordance with the original schedule he had set for himself. President John Witherspoon elected not to be bullied by a thirteen-year-old

No explanation for Aaron Burr's indifference to the American cause has ever been offered, either in his own time or subsequently. His attitude is one of the mysteries that have made him an enigma for more than two hundred years.

His undergraduate essays, which reflected his personal interests, were written on such themes as "honor" and "the passions," and the most ambitious of his papers, which he submitted in his philosophy course, was called "The Origins of Idolatry." In none of these works did he display any particular talent as an original thinker or writer, but his overall scholarship could not be faulted. It was the custom for faculty members to vote on the relative scholastic merits of members of the graduating class, and Aaron won first place in English literature and oratory, first in philosophy, second in Latin, and second in Greek. He was graduated *summa cum laude* at the age of sixteen.

Meanwhile, Burr was already acquiring a name for himself as something of an iconoclast among his contemporaries. A religious revival movement was sweeping through the Colonies, but he scoffed at it, and even his friends were shocked. Had it not been for his ancestry, his attitudes might have remained unnoticed, but Americans of every class were startled when they learned that the grandson of the renowned Reverend Jonathan Edwards was a freethinker who questioned the existence of God. It is significant that Burr's stand was no mere pose taken by an adolescent for the purpose of upsetting his elders. His beliefs were consistent, and although he never crusaded on their behalf, he remained a freethinker for the rest of his life.

On his sixteenth birthday he inherited the considerable sum of ten thousand pounds from the estate of his father, the equivalent of seventy to eighty thousand dollars two centuries later, and was no longer financially dependent upon Timothy Edwards. Acting on his own initiative, he enrolled in a Pennsylvania academy for theologians directed by the Reverend Dr. Joseph Bellamy, who trained freethinker graduate students for the clergy.

Burr's attendance at the school quickly cured him of any desire to spend his life in the pulpit. He developed a strong animosity to Dr. Bellamy and within a few months came close to rejecting all organized religion. Bored by the academy, he decided to turn instead to the law, and undoubtedly influenced by Tapping Reeve, now his brother-in-law, he went to Connecticut and enrolled in Reeve's Litchfield Law School.

His intellect was so prodigious that he found it necessary to devote only a small fraction of his time to his studies and paid far more attention to the young ladies of the area. One with whom he enjoyed a short-lived romance was Dolly Quincy, of Fairfield, soon to become the wife of a young Boston merchant and shipowner, John Hancock, reputedly one of the wealthiest men in the New World. Hancock, already active in the Patriot cause and soon to become the most powerful man in the Continental Congress, was jealous of Aaron Burr for the rest of his life. His enmity may have been partly responsible for the lack of support shown in Congress, in the late 1770s, for the campaign launched by the supporters of Colonel Aaron Burr, who sought for him the rank of brigadier general.

Certainly Burr had no one but himself to blame for Hancock's dislike. The lovely Dolly was already betrothed when Aaron entered her life, but he allowed none of the properties to stand in the way of what he wanted, and over a period of several months he paid assiduous court to the girl. Whether he would have married her himself had he been given the opportunity is a question that has never been answered.

Dolly's family gave her no chance to change her mind, and she was sent off to Boston to become John Hancock's bride before the persistent Aaron Burr could create a scandal.

No one who knew the young law student, however, blamed Dolly Quincy for her infatuation with him. Although the slender Aaron, at five feet, five and one-half inches in height, was about three inches shorter than the average for the period, he was incomparably handsome, and his vibrant personality more than made up for his size. His large, impassioned eyes reflected every nuance of his many changes of mood, his smile was dazzling, and he had become an accomplished and witty conversationalist. Men either were immediately drawn to him or exhibited an aversion to him, whereas women of all ages found him irresistible.

According to contemporary accounts, he did not walk but swaggered. His manners were elaborate and courtly, and his sense of humor was devastating. Somewhere along the way he had learned to wear clothes with a sense of style, and even when carelessly attired, he gave the impression of being a dandy. He was seldom careless in his dress, however, spending considerable sums on his wardrobe, and he was always conscious of his effect on others. This tendency, which grew more pronounced as he matured, became one of the principal character weaknesses that caused his undoing.

Law school and a variety of flirtations continued to occupy Aaron's time in 1773 and 1774, and if he was aware of the so-called Boston Massacre and the Boston Tea Party, propaganda triumphs engineered by the cunning Samuel Adams, his correspondence with various classmates does not indicate it.

No Colonial could have failed to be conscious of the momentous events that shook America in the spring of 1775, however. A British army of occupation held Boston, shots were exchanged between Redcoats and Colonial irregulars at Lexington and Concord, and the American War of Independence began. The Patriots performed a miracle by standing up to the enemy at the Battle of Bunker Hill, and the Continental Congress, which assumed control of the nation's destinies, summoned a Virginia planter, George Washington, and gave him command of the forces gathering at Cambridge, Massachusetts, for the purpose of expelling the Redcoats from Boston.

Regardless of whether Aaron Burr entertained strong feelings about American independence, his active nature would not permit him to remain idle in a fight. Dolly Hancock's influence won him and his friend Mathias Ogden a letter of introduction to General Washington from John Hancock, and Aaron hurried off to Cambridge, eager for action and, according to a long letter he wrote to Sally Reeve, certain he would win glory.

In the long weeks that followed he was doomed to suffer crushing disappointment for the first time in his near-adult life.

Chapter 2

Only the few Americans who had served in the Royal Army or had fought with the British in the French and Indian Wars recognized the magnitude of the task facing Major General George Washington. His supplies of arms, ammunition, uniforms, and other essentials were limited, and his volunteers were totally lacking in military experience, yet he was facing one of the best-trained, best-equipped forces on earth. Every educated man, every financially solvent volunteer, who came to his Cambridge camp expected to be given a high commission and the command of troops, but only a tiny handful were qualified for such posts.

So the Commander-in-Chief was somewhat less than overjoyed when Aaron Burr and his friend Matt Ogden appeared at his headquarters in July, 1775, and presented him with their letter of introduction from John Hancock. Ever courteous, Washington treated them politely but made it plain that there were no commissions available. They had two alternatives: They could enlist in the Continentals, the new national army, perhaps in the militia of Massachusetts or Connecticut or New Jersey, or they could await developments in the hope that openings might be found.

Ogden promptly used other influence and within a few weeks was given a commission as a major. Other friends, some of them even younger than the nineteen-year-old Aaron, had been made captains and lieutenants, but Burr had already used his only reserves of influence. The jealous Hancock would do no more for him, Tapping Reeve had no significant contacts in military circles, and Aaron had never made the acquaintance of the generals and colonels whose brigades and regiments were training in the Massachusetts hills for their assault on the British in Boston.

The idea of enlisting as a private did not cross Aaron Burr's mind, and if anyone suggested to him that he join the Continentals at the bottom of the ladder, he promptly rejected the notion. He was a gentleman, the son of a gentleman, a college graduate who would soon be qualified to practice law, and either he would obtain a commission or he would not fight. Since he had no intention of missing the fame and adventure the war promised, he decided to wait for the opening that General Washington had mentioned in such vague terms. Meanwhile, he decided to enjoy himself in Cambridge, so he found comfortable lodgings, made it his business to meet a number of attractive young ladies, and idled away his days entertaining and being entertained.

As the weeks passed and he saw his friends winning commissions, he became increasingly perturbed. His letters to Sally Reeve during this period reveal his mounting anxiety, spurred by the fear that the war would end before he could snatch his share of glory. His correspondence, however, exhibits no real understanding of the magnitude of the task that faced the Americans, military and civilian, and it appears that he did not look beyond the personal role he hoped to play in the conflict.

Every morning and afternoon Aaron visited the headquarters of the Commander-in-Chief, and on each occasion he was given the same dreary reply to his request: No commissions were available. The hatred he felt for General Washington stems from this time. Subsequently, in letter after letter he criticized the Virginian, insisting to Sally and Tapping that others, notably Charles Lee and Horatio Gates, both of whom had served in the Royal Army, were better qualified for the American command.

In the latter part of August Burr went to bed for several days after being stricken with what he called a nervous fever. In all probability he suffered a mild attack of smallpox, which was decimating the American camp at this time. He suffered no permanent ill effects, but his ailment almost caused him to lose his chance for the action he so desperately sought.

Just as he left his sickbed he learned that more than twelve hundred volunteers had left Massachusetts under the command of one of the few authentic heroes the war had yet produced — Colonel Benedict Arnold. Chagrin overwhelmed the youth, in part because Arnold was one of a small number of American leaders who had won his admiration. A shrewd strategist and brilliant tactician, Benedict Arnold was a self-taught soldier, a man endowed with unlimited personal courage and an instinct for war. It was rumored that his expedition intended to capture Quebec City and the little town of Montreal and thus rob the British of their Canadian base.

Burr immediately made up his mind to allow nothing to interfere with his joining the expedition. Two of his ancestors had played prominent roles in the capture of French forts during the French and Indian Wars, and his own instinct told him this was his golden opportunity. Although debilitated by his illness, he set out on foot for Newburyport, thirty miles from Cambridge, where Arnold's force was embarking on troop transports.

According to a persistent but unverified story that has survived down to the present day, Timothy Edwards sent his servant to intercept Aaron, being convinced that the long walk would kill the youth. Aaron refused to turn back, however, and threatened to lop off the servant's head with his sword if the man tried to force his return.

Arriving in Newburyport before the transports sailed, Aaron enlisted the aid of Matt Ogden and Samuel Spring, both of whom were officers assigned to the force. Colonel Arnold approved of the fervor of the exhausted young man and accepted him provisionally, warning him that he would not be granted a commission until his health improved and would be returned to Cambridge as a civilian if he failed to make a complete recovery.

The ships sailed up the Atlantic Coast to the Kennebec River, in the Maine District of Massachusetts, then headed upstream as far as they could travel. Thereafter the men marched overland to Fort Western, a supply depot that had been a stronghold for more than a quarter of a century. The seas had been rough, and the overland march had not been easy, but Aaron Burr had benefited from both the voyage and the hike through the forests, and his health was restored by the time the corps reached the fort.

During the better part of September, while the troops remained at Fort Western making final preparations for their long push northward, Burr found many ways to call himself to Colonel Arnold's attention. He displayed a zeal for making himself useful, and before leaving for the march through the wilderness at the beginning of the last week in September, Benedict Arnold gave him a brevet, or temporary commission, as an ensign, the lowest rank of commissioned officer. If Burr was unhappy because he had not been awarded a higher rank, he made no complaint.

The corps traveled by water whenever possible, using bateaux the men had fashioned at Fort Western, and when forced to march overland in places where the rivers were too narrow, the heavy craft were carried. At first the expedition enjoyed balmy weather, and there was no lack of food; berries were plentiful, rivers and lakes were filled with fish, and the forest abounded with game. Then, almost overnight, conditions changed: Fish and game vanished, and there were grim portents of the winter awaiting the men on their northward march.

For a century and a half pioneers had been waging a struggle for survival in the seemingly endless forests of North America. The wilderness was the harshest of enemies, and only a few of the hardiest explorers and colonists, trappers and hunters and immigrants, had successfully pitted themselves against nature. Without exception only men who truly enjoyed outdoor life were at home in the vast "sea of trees," as it had been called by generation after generation of adventures.

Aaron Burr belonged to the most sophisticated class of Americans and not only had enjoyed civilized luxuries from birth, but had spent virtually all of his nineteen years as a student living in comfortable surroundings. He was unacquainted with forest travel, knew nothing about woods lore, and had never demonstrated any interest in hunting or fishing. So it appeared almost inevitable that he would be miserable on the long march and would be one of the first to succumb to the many ailments that caused Arnold to lose one fourth of his force in a scant three weeks.

Burr, however, surprised everyone, himself excepted, and thrived on wilderness living. For the first time in his nineteen years he was being challenged by a primitive force, and he met the test. His ability to absorb information was invaluable, and he learned so much about the forest — where to find medicinal herbs, how to make a bed of boughs and place it on high ground, how to detect the sounds of running water in the distance, how to find game when virtually none was available — that he became one of the corps's experts on the wilderness by the time the survivors of the expedition reached Quebec. Painfully thin when he had left Cambridge, he grew even thinner, but he made no complaint when the entire command was placed on half-rations, and he appeared tireless at the end of a long day's grueling march.

Although a commission had been the price he had demanded in return for his service, he did not hesitate to share the work of his men. He took his place in the line for hours at a time carrying the heavy canoes. He searched for firewood and dug trenches, and no task was too menial for him. Knowing many of his troops were ill, he performed many of their individual chores and thus won their admiration. Colonel Arnold himself made a brief notation in his journal to the effect that Ensign Burr's men were willing to follow wherever he chose to lead them.

In mid-October three hundred men and their officers deserted en masse and returned to Massachusetts. A week later a hurricane devastated the forest and ruined what was left of the corps's precious supplies. Several members of the high command advocated turning back, but Benedict Arnold refused and persuaded the remaining troops to go on with him by presenting them with the dubious argument that they were now closer to Quebec than they were to Cambridge. Ensign Aaron Burr was the first member of his battalion to volunteer his continuing services on the endless northward march toward Quebec, the strongest fortress in North America, where General Sir Guy Carleton awaited his attackers with a powerful army of Redcoats and Indian warriors.

The overnight transformation of Aaron Burr, a pampered civilian, classics student, and law scholar, into a soldier and leader of men is one of the most dramatic of the chameleonlike changes that marked his extraordinary life. It should be remembered that he had received no military training and that his studies of the campaigns of Julius Caesar and Alexander the Great constituted his only reading on the subject. He had never held a position of responsible authority over others, and he was making his first trip into the wilderness. In spite of all these handicaps, however, he soon became the most efficient junior officer in the corps, as the logs and dispatches of his superiors repeatedly indicate.

One of the more fascinating developments of the march is the growing rapport of Burr and Colonel Benedict Arnold. In a little more than a quarter of a century these two men would be regarded as the twin arch-villains of the infant United States of America, and the names of both would become synonymous with treason. It is small wonder that they understood each other and for a time created mutual bonds of sympathy; if they were not birds of a feather, at least they shared many personality traits.

Both were courageous to a fault, and both were boundlessly ambitious and caught up in dreams of glory. Self-taught soldiers, they were military geniuses, but Arnold's talents were limited to the sphere of waging war. In all other realms he was woefully lacking in judgment, and although thin-skinned himself, was callously indifferent to the feelings of others.

Burr's abilities covered a far broader spectrum. As he would demonstrate in the years ahead, he would become a superb administrator, a great politician, a first-rate lawyer, and a manipulator of men without parallel in his time. He too, was hypersensitive to the reactions of others, and although he could be as ruthless as Arnold in trampling on someone else

25

when his own interests were at stake, he was more subtle in his dealings with people.

Many years later the taciturn Brigadier General Daniel Morgan, of Virginia, leader of the renowned Morgan's Rifles, commented on their differences, having come to know both of them intimately during the Quebec campaign, in which he served initially as a captain. Arnold, he stated, would carve out the heart of any man who stood in his way, but Burr would smile at his enemy, speak quietly to him, and after the man lowered his guard, slit his throat.

Certainly the march into Canada gave Aaron Burr his first real opportunity to study Americans of classes other than his own. He had been reared and schooled as a member of the intellectual aristocracy, the one group with whom he felt at home throughout his long life. As he learned about others, however, he developed a remarkable talent for dealing with people on their own level. Never condescending, even though he privately considered himself a cut above them, he was able to speak their language and almost always succeeded in creating the impression that he shared their problems and aspirations. Most of the men who served under him on the Quebec campaign were unaware that he held a *summa cum laude* degree from the College of New Jersey, that he was fluent in four languages besides English, or that he read philosophical treatises for the sheer pleasure of exercising his intellect.

Burr needed his physical stamina and courage and his intellectual prowess and cunning to survive the long march. Other men, taller and huskier and stronger, died of illness, cold, and starvation. Snow came early to Canada, most of the expedition's bateaux were smashed in the St. Lawrence River, and Colonel Arnold lost most of his remaining supplies. Medicines were scarce, the sick were left to die in the wilderness, and healthy men, afraid they would suffer the same fate if they fell ill, deserted in large numbers.

By the time Arnold's battered, ragged corps reached the outskirts of Quebec late in November and stared across the St. Lawrence at the great fort resting on the crest of a high cliff, the twelve hundred volunteers had been reduced to a force of about five hundred. The survivors were in high spirits, however, ready to follow Arnold anywhere; their hardships had transformed farm boys and town clerks into real soldiers, and they were confident they could carry out their mission.

A second American force, commanded by Brigadier General Richard Montgomery, had already reached Canada by an easier route, and surprising the British, had captured a number of small outposts. According to rumors that Arnold picked up from farmers and stray frontier travelers, Montgomery had also taken Montreal, then a fur-trading town of about four thousand persons. It was essential that he establish immediate liaison with the general and obtain the assistance of Montgomery's men for the climactic assault on Quebec.

This was more easily said than done. Arnold's messenger had to travel alone, in the dead of winter, through 179 miles of the Canadian wilderness from Quebec to Montreal, all of it territory under British control and patrolled by roving bands of Indian warriors who were Britain's allies. Even if the miraculous feat should be accomplished, there was no guarantee that Arnold's dispatch-carrier would find Montgomery at Montreal. The rumors about the general might prove false, in which event it would be necessary to locate him elsewhere in the wilderness.

Arnold realized the task would have to be performed by someone who was resourceful and shrewd as well as courageous and unhesitatingly gave the seemingly impossible assignment to Ensign Aaron Burr. The latter's friends felt certain they would never see him again, but he eagerly accepted the order, and after paying a brief visit to a nearby farmhouse, where a priest had died a day or two earlier, he set out on his mission.

His scheme was almost unbelievably bold: He had disguised himself as a priest, carrying a brace of pistols and a short sword beneath his cassock. The most direct route to Montreal was by way of the St. Lawrence River, but he knew he could not negotiate the rapids alone, especially when moving upstream, so he headed inland, following trails when he could, then making his way through the deep, snow-blanketed forests.

Settlers gave Burr refuge on his first three nights, directing him on his journey before he departed the next morning. He addressed them in French, speaking the language so well, without an accent, that he aroused no suspicions. Later, in boasting of his exploit, he also admitted that he amused himself by speaking in Latin from time to time, quoting from the *Orations* of Cicero. Twice he encountered small bands of Ottawa braves, but the savages treated him courteously, and one group made him a gift of several dried fish before they parted company.

On his fourth night Burr reached a wilderness monastery, a collection of log huts set deep in the forests, and brazenly maintaining his disguise, spent the night and part of the next day there. His talents as an actor were sufficient to impress the monks, and not only did they fail to penetrate his disguise, but when he departed, they offered him the services of a guide.

Within this man's help Burr made far better time on the wilderness road, and in another two and a half days he saw the log palisades of Montreal in the distance. The guide left him after expressing fears for his safety, saying the American rebels had taken possession of the town. This was all Burr needed to know, and the American soldiers on sentinel duty were astonished when a robed priest emerged from the forest, spoke to them in their own tongue, and demanded that he be taken without delay to General Montgomery.

The general was even more surprised when the "priest" saluted, reached inside his cassock, and produced two long communications from Colonel Arnold. Not even an ambitious young romantic who had been filled with dreams of glory could have asked for a more dramatic, satisfying scene. The mission had been a complete success.

Chapter 3

Brigadier General Richard Montgomery was a hearty man with a lively imagination and a quick appreciation of the talents of others. Deeply impressed by Ensign Aaron Burr's exploit, he immediately promoted the young man to the rank of captain, jumping him two grades, and assigned him to a post on his own headquarters staff. For the immediate moment Aaron's hopes were fulfilled. Not yet twenty years old, he had attained a respectable rank, and even more important, as a member of General Montgomery's staff he attended meetings of the American high command and consequently would have a voice in the planning of future operations.

Montgomery and Arnold joined forces early in December, 1775. Subsequently, long councils of war were held to determine the nature of the attack to be made on the fortress of Quebec. Arnold favored the most audacious of the plans, and Captain Aaron Burr also voted in favor of it. The basic scheme was as simple as it was hazardous.

The so-called Cape Diamond blockhouse was the defense point located at the highest place within the British walls and consequently housed fewer defenders than other bastions. Therefore it was proposed that a special American force be trained in the use of scaling ladders. On the night of the next snowfall, when the elements would obscure American movements, a diversionary assault would be made elsewhere on the great fort's wall. While the British were distracted, the special Colonial force would climb into the Cape Diamond blockhouse, turn the cannon there on the enemy, and open the gates to the main American body.

It was obvious that everything would depend upon the men selected for the perilous mission, their training, and their leadership. Captain Aaron Burr, recognizing the chance to redouble his renown in a single night's battle, offered to command the special force. Montgomery and Arnold, the co-commanders, had complete faith in him and accepted without further discussion. Aaron was also given the privilege of personally selecting the fifty members of his special troop.

For the next week Burr drilled his men incessantly in the use of ladders, and the exercises were performed from sunrise until dusk. Then, while the men dropped exhausted onto their pallets to sleep, Aaron slipped away to scout the enemy positions. He roamed where he pleased until the small hours of the morning, often sneaking inside the British sentry lines so he could familiarize himself with the terrain.

But nature refused to cooperate with the Americans. No snow fell, so the co-commanders, afraid to tarry too long, changed their plans. The attack would be launched on the town of Quebec, located directly below the fort. It was argued that the inhabitants, many of them merchants, would capitulate without delay rather than see their property and shops, warehouses and homes, destroyed. The town, like the great citadel itself, was protected by a high wall, and the members of the war council decided after protracted debate that the best entrance for their purposes was located at the upper end of the civilian community, where a gate stood at the end of a narrow passageway, with palisades on each side. A miniature fort guarded the gate, and the Americans were determined to overwhelm the bastion while creating a diversion elsewhere.

Burr had already scouted the civilian gate, and in his opinion the risks were enormous. If the defenders were alert, he explained, they could cut down the attackers, who would be hemmed in on both sides and would be forced to retreat to the mouth of the channel in order to escape. But his superiors approved to the plan in spite of his protests.

Even though he entertained deep misgivings, Aaron immediately volunteered to lead the assault on the gate, and his 50 picked men voted to accompany him. An additional 150 were assigned to follow the vanguard, and the fall of the gate was regarded as so critical that General Montgomery said he would accompany the party himself.

Clouds filtered across the early December sky on the night of the attack, partly concealing the Americans, and Montgomery's artillery opened a bombardment on schedule. Colonel Arnold feinted to draw the full attention of the British defenders from the gate that was so vital to the American plan, simulating a major assault against the far side of the fort, while several of Burr's men quickly sawed through a palisade. The first two men who moved into the narrow corridor between the log walls that led to the gate were General Montgomery and Captain Burr.

They crept forward, their men close behind them, and Montgomery muttered, "In two more minutes, Quebec will be ours."

His words were the last he ever spoke. The Redcoats had not been fooled by the attackers' ruse, and waiting, until the last possible moment, the troops stationed in the miniature fort opened up with a murderous musket and artillery fire. General Montgomery was cut down, dying instantly, and scores of other Americans were killed, too. In a matter of a few seconds Captain Aaron Burr found himself the only living man facing the enemy.

The entire corridor was littered with the dead and dying, and those who had been moving into the channel between the high log walls were unable to retreat, precisely as Burr had predicted. The only escape route was choked, and the carnage was beyond description.

Aaron Burr's reaction to the situation was one of the most astonishing performances of personal heroism recorded in all of the annals of the American War of Independence. It was a miracle that he had not been hit and equally miraculous that he did not lose his head. He was so close to the miniature fort that he could almost reach out and touch the enemy guns, and he was convinced that the post could be reduced by a storming party.

Jumping to his feet and waving his sword, he tried to rally the surviving Americans for a rush on the enemy position. Not one man responded to his summons, however, because the steady British fire kept even the bravest from the entrance to the corridor.

Still unmarked by British bullets, Burr finally realized the cause was hopeless. So he turned, picked up the heavy, lifeless body of General Montgomery, and started to make his way back along the corridor. This act of unselfish courage so overwhelmed the Redcoats that they paid him the supreme compliment of holding their fire until he reached safety, the general's body still cradled in his arms.

The brief battle ended in complete catastrophe for the Americans. Out of a total force of approximately eleven hundred, two hundred had been either killed or severely wounded and another three hundred had been captured, among them the incomparable Dan Morgan, whose subsequent release was of inestimable benefit to the American cause. Benedict Arnold himself had suffered a painful but minor injury when he was cut down by a stray British bullet.

Aaron was adamant in his insistence that Quebec could have been taken if the men at the rear of the corridor had pushed forward instead of retreating. His report was worded in such strong terms that it resulted in a complete reshuffle of what was left of the high command.

The wounded Colonel Arnold, who would receive word of his promotion to brigadier general in a few weeks, singled out Captain Burr for the highest praise in his dispatches to General Washington and to the Continental Congress. The survivors of the abortive attack voted the lieutenant colonel who had ordered the retreat out of office and unanimously recommended that Captain Burr be promoted to brigade major to replace him. Benedict Arnold signed the order that same day.

The story of the disaster increased the gloom of the Patriots at home, and the people were hungry for crumbs of good news. So the accounts of Aaron's deeds provided at least a measure of solace, and almost overnight he became the most famous of the fighting men in the Continental Army. The Continental Congress applauded speech after speech praising him, the newspapers in all thirteen of the Colonies called him the greatest hero in the land, and General Washington, always reserved, wrote him a warm letter of commendation.

Meanwhile, the siege of Quebec continued. Arnold's force, reduced to a mere three hundred, after Montgomery's corps returned to Montreal, spent the entire winter within sight of the Canadian citadel. Reinforcements finally arrived in March and April, bringing badly needed provisions and arms with them. General Arnold was determined to renew the attack and still spoke in terms of capturing Quebec, but his brigade major, perhaps the most important member of his staff, heartily disagreed with him.

Twenty-year-old Aaron Burr had learned much about the science and art of waging war and was convinced the Americans had lost their chance to take the citadel. The British garrison was receiving reinforcements of men, supplies, and munitions, and the American besiegers could do nothing to prevent their delivery by ships that crossed the Atlantic at will and cast anchor at the foot of the huge fortress. A number of warships were arriving, too, to aid in the defense of the city, and Burr, who had become eminently practical in such matters, believed that the hope of reducing the fortress was nothing but a dream.

His differences with General Arnold became sharper in the early months of the spring. He wrote to friends that Benedict Arnold was a great tactician and leader of men in combat but that he lacked the capacity for strategic planning essential in an independent commander, a judgment that history has verified. The Canadian venture was a lost cause, in Aaron's opinion, and he began to seek action elsewhere.

Mathias Ogden was trying to obtain a position for him on General Washington's personal staff, and Aaron had every reason to believe he would win the appointment. The British having evacuated Boston, the Commander-in-Chief had transferred his base of operations to New York, and friends wrote to Aaron that an army of twenty thousand men, the largest ever gathered by the Patriots, was assembling there. Opportunities for further promotions and fresh laurels awaited the brave, especially those who had the sense to be in the right place at the right time.

Whether Major Aaron Burr received permission from General Benedict Arnold to terminate his service with the expedition or whether he brazenly deserted after being refused permission to leave is a question that has never been resolved.

According to one account, Arnold found his subordinate packing his belongings and ordered him to remain, but Burr refused, saying the general would be required to use force to keep him in Canada. On the other hand, Burr wrote to Sally Reeve that he was returning home on pubic business. His detractors, trying to prove his alleged desertion, have claimed that nowhere in the expedition's records is he mentioned as a messenger, but this omission is meaningless. Records of the brigade's business were informal, and any one of a number of assignments could have been given to the impatient young officer.

Whatever the situation may have been, several facts are clear: Burr left his superior's camp in early May, 1776, and thereafter was never again on good terms with General Arnold. He was one of a very few men who ever disliked Arnold after serving under him.

Returning home by way of Lake Ticonderoga, he stopped off for a few days in Connecticut to visit his sister and brother-in-law, taking advantage of the pause to have a full set of splendid uniforms made for himself. The hero of the Battle of Quebec had no intention of appearing at the headquarters of the Commander-in-Chief wearing shabby, wilderness-stained clothing.

Early in June the resplendent Major Burr reported to General Washington in New York Town and was delighted to discover he had been assigned a post as military secretary to the Commander-in-Chief. His pleasure ebbed considerably, however, when he learned that his principal duties consisted of making fair copies of the general's letters to the Congress and various subordinate commanders. His respect for Washington declined when he discovered that the general's spelling and punctuation were faulty, and the work soon became tedious and dull.

In an attempt to relieve his boredom he made a study of the strategic military situation, reaching the conclusion that New York could not be defended against a combined Royal Navy and Army attack. Acting on his own initiative, he submitted a report to that effect to his superior, recommending that the Patriots burn the city to the ground, retreat into the interior, and force the enemy to fight them there.

Burr had no way of knowing that precisely such a plan had already been considered and rejected. The United States was on the verge of formally declaring her independence, but many people were reluctant to terminate their ties to the mother country, and the leaders of the Continental Congress had persuaded Washington that the burning of the nation's third largest city would be regarded by many Americans as such a ruthless act that they would join the Tory forces.

Convinced that his plan was brilliant, Burr confidently waited for his superior to praise him — and to adopt the scheme. When Washington did neither, the young major began to urge his cause verbally and was so persistent that the general finally became annoyed. He had no time, he wrote, to instruct "beardless boys" in the intricacies of national policies, and from that time he treated his new military secretary with a greater reserve.

The ambitious, impatient Burr quickly realized he had made a mistake when he had accepted his appointment to the Commander-in-Chief's staff. Certainly he had no intention of wasting his time as a clerk or being deprived of a voice in the country's military councils. Few officers had seen field experience that equaled his, and his exploits in Canada spoke for themselves. So he did not hesitate to use the influence he had accumulated to secure another assignment that would give him greater opportunities to win advancement and build his reputation.

John Hancock, who no longer regarded Burr as a romantic rival, was inclined to think of him now as a protégé whose heroic deeds reflected favorably on his own judgment. Sally Reeve had become the close friend of Dolly Hancock, who frequently spent long periods in Connecticut while her husband's duties as President of the Congress kept him in Philadelphia, and Aaron Burr did not hesitate to use either his sister's influence or the goodwill with Hancock that he himself had accumulated. After preparing the President via the ladies, he sent Hancock a letter, stating in the humblest of terms that he sought greater action on behalf of his country than was available to him in his post as a military secretary.

John Hancock, meanwhile, was spending a minimum of eighteen hours each day at his desk, and Sam Adams was the authority for the observation that the President had discovered the secret of how to survive without sleep. But Hancock either made or found the time to take care of Aaron's request. As a result, after serving only two weeks at George Washington's headquarters, Major Burr was transferred to the staff of General Israel Putnam.

A onetime tavern-owner and the father of a large brood of children, the hearty, semiliterate Putnam enjoyed the company of bright young subordinates, to whom he gave as much authority as they could tolerate. Aaron was welcomed boisterously at the Manhattan headquarters of Putnam's division. Here he encountered kindred spirits who enjoyed debating philosophy far into the night. He also found time, during the hot summer months of 1776, to fall in love for the first time in his life.

The girl was Margaret Moncrieffe, who was related to Aaron's late mentor, General Montgomery. The daughter of a British major of marines, she had been inadvertently left behind when her father had been summoned to duty with the British fleet now on patrol off the shores of Manhattan Island. She had been semi-adopted by Mrs. Putnam, and at the age of fourteen, then regarded as relatively mature, she was a beauty. Aaron saw her daily at the Putnam house, and the two young romantics were soon drawn to each other.

Little is known about their relationship, but it is assumed they were serious and perhaps wished to be married. But General and Mrs. Putnam had no desire to accept responsibility for such an important step when the girl was not their own child, and eventually they were compelled to take appropriate action. One day in early August a small American brig sailed into the midst of the great British ships of the line and frigates under a flag of truce, and Margaret was delivered, with due ceremony, to Admiral Richard Howe, the British sea commander.

She was reunited with her father that same day and dropped out of Aaron's life. As, nearly as can be gleaned, he did not mourn her departure, having already reached the independent conclusion that he was not yet prepared to settle down with a wife. The romance, however, heightened by the news of the method chosen for Margaret's return to her father, won him the reputation of being a ladies' man, and men still coupled his name with that of Margaret a half century later.

Meanwhile, the American troops had far more important matters to consider. On August 22 the brother of Admiral Lord Howe, British army commander General William Howe, soon to be knighted, landed a large force on Long Island. Washington dispatched the bulk of his small army to meet and repel the invaders, and the ensuing Battle of Long Island developed into the worst American debacle of the war.

Aaron Burr was sent forward to inspect the breastworks erected in the farmlands of Brooklyn by the advance guard of his division and reported to General Putnam that they were inadequate to protect the troops. He recommended that the division either move forward and attack the enemy without delay or draw back to stronger positions. General Putnam, however, was unwilling to move without the express approval of the Commander-in-Chief, and the day's ensuing events did not cause Aaron to revise his low opinion of General Washington.

The superbly trained Redcoats and the Hessian mercenaries who came ashore with them were professional soldiers led by officers who had spent their entire adult lives in uniform. They faced awkward country boys and pallid city dwellers who had no understanding of even the fundamentals of warfare. In addition, most of the American officers, drawn largely from the Colonies' tiny patrician class, were as ignorant as their men. The results were inevitable, and the carnage was frightful.

Again and again in the heat of battle the Americans became panicky and retreated in wild disorder. Flanks were exposed repeatedly, allowing the enemy to strike at will where they pleased. Eventually the Redcoats regarded the engagement as a joke, and regimental buglers played hunting calls as the efficient cavalry led one sweeping charge after another.

Alexander the Great had once declared that any fool could lead an attack but that the true soldier proved his worth by his conduct during a retreat. Major Aaron Burr may have remembered the observation when he was assigned the command of Putnam's rear guard and ordered to protect the withdrawal of the division to Manhattan Island. If Alexander was right, there could have been no question that Aaron Burr was a soldier. He rode incessantly up and down the lines of his ragged infantrymen, exhorting and cursing, leading them by example as he recklessly exposed himself to enemy fire. Alternately inspiring and threatening his men, he forced them to maintain some semblance of order, and Putnam's troops managed to complete their disengagement with fewer casualties and desertions than most units.

There was little that was favorable in the retreat, and a weary General Putnam reserved his only words of praise, in his report to the Commander-in-Chief, for the courage and the skill of Major Burr.

The desperate Patriots enjoyed no respite. General Howe followed them from Long Island to Manhattan, and had he not hesitated, perhaps to regroup, what remained of Washington's disorganized forces could have been destroyed. In theory the tactics being employed by the Redcoats were sound, and only a delay in their execution made it possible for the still retreating Americans to escape.

Aaron Burr managed to add to his laurels during the hasty withdrawal. Howe landed a strong contingent of troops at Murray's Hill, hoping to cut his enemy's forces in half, but he was so tardy in setting up his lines that most of the Patriot units managed to escape northward before the British closed their trap. One brigade of General Putnam's division had not yet deployed to a position north of Murray's Hill, however, and Putnam gave young Major Burr the unenviable assignment of trying to lead the troops to safety.

Riding south with two junior officers, Burr located the brigade and was horrified to discover that its officers had ordered the men to construct breastworks. Already virtually surrounded by the British, the brigade's leaders had decided to make a stand. Common sense indicated the stupidity of their decision: Six hundred Patriots were being sealed off by thousands of Redcoats, and no matter how great their valor, there was literally no chance they would win a battle. Within an hour or two they would be overwhelmed, and those who were not killed or wounded would undoubtedly be captured.

The Quebec campaign had taught Burr the futility of false heroics. Standing in his saddle, he waved his sword and ordered the brigade to follow him. Two troops of British cavalry and a reinforced battalion of Redcoat infantry stood between him and safety, so he smashed through their lines, driving with such fury that the solid enemy phalanx was destroyed.

Not only was the daring maneuver successful, enabling the entire brigade to rejoin Washington's main body, but the Redcoats who had tried to cut off the unit were put to flight. Burr inflicted heavy casualties, captured a number of prisoners, and had the grim satisfaction of knowing that in the overall battle he alone had forced the enemy to retreat.

Of far greater significance was a letter that he sent to Timothy Edwards on the eve of the Battle of Long Island. The lengthy, unhurried communication, written in a neat hand, was almost uncannily prophetic. Burr described, in precise detail, each move that General Howe would make, first on Long Island, then on Manhattan. The British had followed his blueprint without deviation. It was small consolation, however, to realize he had the perspicacity to anticipate British planning. The defeat of the Patriots was too great.

Aaron Burr remained with Putnam's division on the retreat southward through New Jersey and into Pennsylvania, but he did not give in to despair. On the contrary, he saw the Americans gaining several specific advantages from the new situation, and another letter, which he wrote late in September, reveals the soundness and depth of his thinking:

> We have hitherto opposed them with less than half their number, and exposed to all their advantages of shipping. Our force is now more united, theirs more divided. Our present situation renders their navy of less service to them, and less formidable to us; a circumstance of vast importance, and to which I attribute all that has heretofore appeared in their favor. Add to these, besides confirming our internal union, the effect that every appearance of success on the part of the enemy has upon our leading men. It arouses them from the lethargy which began to prevail; convinces them that their measures are unequal to their grand designs; that the present is the important moment, and that every nerve must now be exerted.

This is not altogether fanciful. It has been actually the case.

The shortage of qualified officers in the Patriot camp had now grown so severe that Burr confidently anticipated a big promotion. At the very least, he wrote to Sally Reeve, he expected to be advanced to the rank of colonel, but it was not too much to hope he might be made a brigadier general.

General Putnam recommended him for a promotion, but the Commander-in-Chief ignored the request, neither approving nor rejecting it. General Washington, himself thin-skinned, remembered that the young major had requested a transfer from his own headquarters, a slight that was difficult to forgive and forget.

Burr was well aware of Washington's antagonism toward him but attributed it, in the main, to the jealousy of one of the Commander-in-Chief's personal aides, Alexander Hamilton. This exceptionally talented young officer had won a place of favor in Washington's official family and guarded it zealously.

He made no secret of his ambitions, and his personality clashed with Aaron's so severely that it is no exaggeration to say their long feud dates from the autumn of 1776 and continued for a quarter of a century until its tragic climax, which marked the beginning of Aaron Burr's downfall. Apparently, their mutual dislike from the outset was chemical; even though it was based on no specific incident or quarrel, it was an ever-present factor in their relationship.

Chapter 4

Frustrated in his hopes of winning a promotion, Major Aaron Burr was occupied with routine tasks: He copied letters and divisional orders, he carried dispatches, and he kept records of staff meetings. Above all, however, he brooded.

His discontent was fanned by the personal circumstances in which he found himself. Putnam's division spent the better part of the winter of 1776-1777 in Princeton, and not only was Aaron quartered in Nassau Hall, which had been his home as an undergraduate, but he slept in the same room he had occupied at the beginning of the decade. Remembering the high ambitions he had entertained, he could not help thinking that he was wasting his substance while other men reaped the rewards of their labors.

His pride did not permit him to complain, much less to request a promotion from higher authority. But it hurt to see men who had been junior to him and whose accomplishments had been far less important than his being raised to higher positions. He kept silent until March, 1777, when he revealed something of what he felt in a letter to his old friend, Matt Ogden, now a full colonel and soon to be made a brigadier general:

> ... As to "expectations of promotion," I have not the least, either in the line or in the staff. You need not express any surprise at it... 'Tis true indeed that my former equals and even inferiors in rank have left me. Assurances from those in power I have had unasked and in abundance; but of these I shall never remind them.

Washington and Sir William Howe maneuvered incessantly in the early months of 1777, but Aaron saw no action during the spring and early summer and became convinced he had been deliberately shunted aside. Unless he could be of service to his country, he later wrote to his sister, he would prefer to resign his commission, return to civilian life, and complete his studies so he could begin the practice of law.

Finally, on June 29, General Washington promoted him to the rank of lieutenant colonel and assigned him to the line as deputy commander of a Continental regiment. It was a crushing blow not to have been made a full colonel, at the very least, and Burr, unable to contain his feelings any longer, expressed them freely in a letter to the Commander-in-Chief as indiscreet as it was angry:

> I am this morning favored with your excellency's letter of the 29th instant and my appointment to Colonel Malcolm's regiment. Am truly sensible of the honor done me and shall be studious that my deportment in that situation be such as will ensure your future esteem. I am nevertheless, sir, constrained to observe that the late date of my appointment subjects me to the command of many who were younger in the service and junior officers of the last campaign.
>
> With submission and, if there is no impropriety in requesting what so nearly concerns me, I would beg to know whether it was any misconduct in me or any extraordinary merit of service in them, which entitled the gentlemen lately put over me to that preference? If neither be the case, may I not expect to be restored to that rank of which I have been deprived?

General Washington may have regarded the questions as rhetorical. In any event, if he answered the letter, no copy of the reply is extant.

Burr received the promotion at Peekskill, New York, where General Putnam now made his headquarters, and left at once for nearby Orange County, New York, where the regiment, one of those under Putnam's jurisdiction, was stationed. There he discovered that his situation was not as bad as he had feared.

Colonel William Malcolm, his immediate superior, was a wealthy farmer and merchant, who in the manner of the British aristocracy regarded his commission as an honor rather than an active charge. He made it plain to his deputy at their first meeting that he had no intention of leading the troops himself and that he was transferring full responsibility to the younger man.

Burr quickly discovered that the regiment was in a deplorable state. The men had ragged clothes, only a few wore shoes, and the lack of ammunition and other supplies was shocking. He immediately provided funds of his own for uniforms and munitions, and his example inspired Colonel Malcolm to dig into his own purse for the same purpose. Some of the minor officers were so incompetent that Burr promptly discharged eleven of them, replacing them with some of Putnam's line and staff officers whose worth he knew.

Then, tightening discipline, he inaugurated a training program more thorough than any other American regiment had ever experienced. His troops marched and countermarched in the open fields; they spent countless hours drilling with bayonets, and they actually wasted precious ammunition and powder in target practice. The improvement in the unit's efficiency and morale was so great that General Putnam wrote the Commander-in-Chief, saying, "There is no finer regiment in the land."

Burr soon had an opportunity to prove his men's worth. William Tryon, the British Governor of occupied New York, had been leading a reinforced brigade on forays into the nearby countryside, raiding, burning, and terrorizing the inhabitants without fear of reprisals. His latest expedition took him in the direction of Orange County, and Burr received an order from General Putnam, telling him to retire out of range of the superior force.

But Lieutenant Colonel Aaron Burr had not prepared his men for combat only to avoid it, and he had no intention of retreating. Flagrantly disobeying his superior's command, he moved his regiment forward for a clash with Tryon. When his scouts brought word that the enemy was within striking distance, Burr ostensibly halted, knowing that spies would carry word of his seeming hesitation to the British.

That night, at sundown, he was on the move again. When he learned where the Redcoat vanguard had pitched its camp, he personally led the regiment in a surprise assault on the enemy. Tryon's advance guard, consisting of a full battalion, was surrounded, and every Redcoat in the unit was either killed or captured. Burr's regiment, as his unit was now being called, carried out the action without the loss of a single man.

Governor Tryon immediately retreated to New York, where his troops would be protected by the cannon of the Royal Navy ships stationed in the harbor. This withdrawal indicated the basic weakness of the enemy, a fact Burr immediately recognized.

In September Sir William Howe, soon to be replaced by Sir Henry Clinton, defeated Washington in a series of skirmishes and minor engagements — few of which deserved to be called full-scale battles — and occupied Philadelphia with the main force of British and mercenary troops. This victory weakened the British, however, and Tryon had so few troops at his disposal that he could send none to the aid of General John Burgoyne, who was marching south from Canada-in what was designed as a maneuver to cut off New York and New England from the other rebellious Colonies.

Aaron discerned with startling clarity that a successful drive on the weakened Redcoat garrison in New York would deprive the British of their operational base. His own recent experience had demonstrated to him that Tryon was vulnerable, and with British troops occupied in so many other places he estimated that New York could be captured by a relatively small corps.

He wrote, accordingly, to Generals Washington and Putnam, requesting that he be given two thousand men for the purpose and promising that he would accomplish his mission.

Meanwhile, in October General Burgoyne was defeated and captured at the Battle of Saratoga by a force nominally commanded by General Horatio Gates. The real hero of that engagement, however, was General Benedict Arnold, who rallied the Patriots when they faltered and led them to victory.

Some students of welfare, Aaron Burr among them, immediately recognized the significance of Saratoga, subsequently called one of the most important battles in the history of the world. Convinced that his reasoning was correct, Aaron renewed his request for troops to lead an assault on the British at New York.

But General Washington had no troops to spare. His gadfly attempts to harry Clinton were proving unsuccessful, and he was encountering staggering difficulties in his attempts to hold his army together. Food was scarce, supplies of munitions were low, and he was unable to procure new clothing and boots. In fact, many of Washington's men went barefoot or covered their feet with rags. Not only was he unable to mount an offensive of consequence anywhere, but desperately needing the help of trained, efficient units, he ordered Burr's regiment transferred to his own command.

Burr was forced to postpone his dreams of conquest and marched south through New Jersey into Pennsylvania, reaching the main body just in time to provide the rear guard for the retreat after Washington's defeat at Germantown. The regiment accompanied the rest of the force into its winter quarters in what the most optimistic called "the natural fortress" of Valley Forge, Pennsylvania. But Aaron had no intention of allowing his men to share the suffering of the army that winter.

His troops were in better physical condition than most, and thanks to their commander's personal generosity, they were better clad. So Burr's regiment was given the unenviable task of acting as a shield against a British surprise attack. The men were exposed to the elements, and the duty was as boring as it was unpleasant, but the regiment did not starve. British supply caravans traveling between New York and Philadelphia were raided regularly, and members of the regiment had warm blankets, heavy stockings and boots, thick cloaks, and enough to eat. They also captured a munitions train, and after helping themselves to muskets and bayonets, powder and shot, they turned over what was left to the high command.

The members of another regiment, which held an outpost about ten miles from Valley Forge, mutinied against their officers, who were quietly removed from the scene, and the Commander-in-Chief, who did not hesitate to utilize the talents of a man he disliked, gave Colonel Burr the delicate task of restoring discipline. Aaron hurried to the outpost, escorted by his own vanguard company, whose men were unswervingly loyal to him. That night, as a precaution, he had all ammunition and powder secretly removed.

The following morning at dawn he mustered the mutineers in parade formation. As he had anticipated, one of the soldiers leaped forward, leveled his musket at the officer, and urged the others to help him shoot down this representative of authority. Aaron Burr coolly drew his sword and slashed the mutineer's arm so severely that he almost amputated it, then ordered the man to resume his place in the line. That ended the mutiny, and the rebellious unit caused no more problems.

The high command failed to recognize Burr's contribution to the war effort, and his sense of dissatisfaction became worse. But the basic situation was gradually taking a turn for the better, and he was one of the first to realize it. Baron Friedrich von Steuben, of Prussia, arrived to drill the troops until they became a real army, and in the spring the appearance of tens of thousands of shad in the rivers that bounded Valley Forge replenished the exhausted food supplies.

By April Aaron Burr had performed the duties of a full colonel for more than nine months but still did not receive a promotion, and he became so disgruntled that he applied for a transfer to the office of General Horatio Gates, who had become chairman of the Continental Congress Board of War. Gates put in a formal request for his services, but Washington replied bluntly that he could not "conveniently spare" a senior officer at that time. Much as he might personally dislike Colonel Burr, he needed every experienced officer.

Late in the spring the British evacuated Philadelphia, intending to withdraw to New York, and were harried so unmercifully by the Patriots that they halted for a full-scale battle at the town of Monmouth. That fight was the last engagement of consequence in which Aaron Burr fought, and it is significant that although still only a lieutenant colonel, he commanded a complete brigade of three regiments, including his own.

He was assigned a position on one of the wings and was ordered to hold his place in order to prevent the British from flanking the American line. It was customary under such circumstances for the center to engage in the active fighting, and it galled Burr to see Lieutenant Colonel Alexander Hamilton distinguishing himself in combat. But at last his own opportunity came, and he seized it. When a British battalion foundered in a swamp directly in front of his position, he led his own regiment forward, in spite of a murderous Redcoat artillery barrage from the rear. It was his intention to take all three of his regiments into battle, storm the British artillery, and thereby collapse the British flank.

General Washington, however, gave him no chance to operate independently. Afraid that Burr's unauthorized assault would leave his own flank exposed, he sent an aide to order the colonel to withdraw without delay.

Burr had no choice and personally plunged into the swamp to direct the withdrawal. An enemy cannonball knocked him from his horse into the mud, and although he was dazed for the moment, he miraculously escaped serious injury. Remounting, he continued to direct the retreat.

Thereafter he obeyed orders without question, even though he longed to send his troops forward again when the British began to retreat northward. Now was the time, he said in a message to the Commander-in-Chief, to destroy the bulk of Sir Henry Clinton's army. But Washington realized the request was not practical. His own army was exhausted after fighting the enemy to a draw, and it lacked the strength to follow.

Burr was frustrated again but did not allow his fury to interfere with his duty to his men. Other commanders might go off to the nearest tavern or inn after a battle for a hot dinner and a strong drink, but according to his concept, the officer in charge of a unit had a personal responsibility for the welfare of his troops. So he tended the wounded himself, bullying tired physicians and surgeons when they would have called a halt until morning. That task completed, he directed the burial of the dead, and when bone-weary troops faltered, he himself seized a shovel and dug grave after grave.

He did not pause for either rest or food, and by mid-morning of the following day he had been at work without respite for almost forty-eight hours. What he failed to realize was that the blow inflicted on him by the British cannonball had been stunning and that he would have retired to a bed had he heeded the warning symptoms of fatigue that assailed him. Not until he tried to walk from the field did he suffer the consequences. Suddenly attacked by an acute dizzy spell, he collapsed and was unable to rise. The cannonball may not have been responsible, however.

At the age of twenty-two Aaron Burr was suffering from what later generations would call a nervous breakdown. He had endured countless hardships for more than three years of warfare, and his condition was undoubtedly exaggerated by the emotional frustration precipitated by the refusal of his superiors to give him the independent command he had so frequently sought. All he himself knew was that his hands shook, he had no appetite, and it was impossible for him to sleep more than an hour or two each night.

General Washington was aware of his condition and gave him a succession of light assignments. First he was directed to supervise the operations of several espionage agents, whom he sent into New York Town to observe British shipping there, paying particular attention to the number of troop transports that sailed for England. Then he himself went into New York under a flag of truce as an escort for a number of prominent Tories, men for whose safety Washington feared if they remained in Patriot-held territory.

It did not occur to the Commander-in-Chief or anyone else that what the exhausted young officer really needed was complete rest, not merely a lightening of his duties. In fifteen months he had not enjoyed a single day's leave of absence from duty, and even now he was not given a furlough.

His regiment had been sent to West Point, New York, and in September, 1778, he rejoined his men there. Early in January, 1779, he was transferred to White Plains, and unable to rest, he transformed a quiet assignment into one of furious activity. Every day he reviewed the troops under his command, supervised training schedules, and presided at courts-martial. Every night he rode toward the enemy lines and tested their sentry outposts; whenever he found a weakness, he quickly exploited it, and over a period of three months he personally led seventeen raids on these outposts, capturing prisoners, taking munitions and supplies, and generally demoralizing the Redcoats.

He also found — or made — time for some highly personal business. Each day, whenever he could seize an hour, he paid a call on a lady who lived in nearby Paramus. He knew, soon after meeting her in January, that she would become the most important woman in his life.

Chapter 5

Mrs. Theodosia Prevost, ten years the senior of Aaron Burr, was the widow of a British army officer and the sister of two other officers in the Crown's service. She was the mother of five children, the eldest of whom was already a cadet officer in the Royal Army. By no stretch of anyone's imagination, even Burr's, could she be considered beautiful, but she had many compensating qualities.

Mrs. Prevost was warm and maternal and provided a young man of just twenty-three with the mother's love he had never known. She was an intellectual, the most cerebral woman of his acquaintance, and her handsome home, called the Hermitage, boasted a library of more than two thousand books, which was considered mammoth in the eighteenth-century New World. Like Aaron, she was an enthusiastic devotee of François Voltaire, and it was she who introduced him to the works of such iconoclastic reformers as economist Jeremy Bentham and philosopher William Godwin, whose ideas strengthened his own refusal to abide by the concepts of other men.

Theodosia Prevost stood apart from politics, and although some of her neighbors suspected her, for a time, of Tory leanings, by 1779 she was popular in highest Patriot military circles. On one occasion General Washington and Colonel Alexander Hamilton were her guests, and Hamilton called again for more of her sparkling conversation, thereby increasing the bad feelings between him and Aaron Burr. Major James Monroe was also a visitor on several evenings.

Burr fell desperately in love with the lady, but she could not be won with ease, and his military situation compounded his misery. His service was still insignificant, he was still denied a major command, and the promotion for which he longed continued to elude him. He took part, once again with distinction, in the brief action against Governor Tryon, who conducted an abortive campaign against Connecticut, but otherwise he did nothing of particular note.

It was Theodosia who first became convinced that Burr was ill and required the services of a physician. He resisted the idea, insisting that nothing could prevent him from doing his duty, but after several physicians had concurred in the initial diagnosis, he reluctantly agreed to resign his commission. It had become obvious to others as well as to him that his services were not being utilized, and he realized he would not be missed. So, late in 1779, he sent his resignation to General Washington. It was accepted without delay.

Burr's physicians suggested that he spend at least six months doing nothing, but the idea did not appeal to him. In February, 1780, he celebrated his twenty-fourth birthday and felt he had to make up for the time he had lost in military service. It had become evident to him, as it had to other thinking Americans, that the independence of the United States was assured, even though the war continued to drag on, so he directed his planning exclusively toward the postwar years.

He was anxious to persuade Theodosia Prevost to marry him but could not go to her empty-handed. Accordingly, he established himself as an importer and exporter in New Haven, spending his weekdays in business and his weekends visiting the lady of whom he had become enamored. He threw himself into his work with his customary, furious energy, enlisting the aid of the many members of the Burr family who lived in Connecticut. But his efforts were premature. Britain still controlled the seas, and although America received a measure of help from the French fleet, the newly independent nation was finding it exceptionally difficult to engage in overseas trade. Aaron made the unexpected discovery, furthermore, that he was not temperamentally suited for the life of a merchant. His work bored him, and his sense of restlessness increased.

He discussed the problem at length with Theodosia, and she not only encouraged him to follow his natural inclinations and become an attorney but promised to marry him as soon as he established himself as a lawyer.

With this goad spurring him, in February, 1781, Burr entered the law offices of his friend, Judge William Paterson, in Raritan, New Jersey. Because Paterson insisted that a candidate observe the letter of the law and spend three years studying before being admitted to the bar, Aaron moved to Haverstraw and began to read in the offices of another friend, Thomas Smith. Three years was far too long for a young man in a hurry to wait.

Demonstrating his usual ability to assimilate vast quantities of knowledge very quickly, Burr made such rapid progress that by the latter part of the same year he had virtually completed the requirements for the bar that were stipulated in most states. Early in December the New York legislature passed a bill disbarring all lawyers who had Tory sympathies, and Aaron saw opportunity beckoning. There would be a shortage of attorneys in New York now, so it was possible he might be admitted to the bar without delay.

He made a hurried trip to Albany and did not hesitate to enlist the aid of various prominent persons in his cause. General Philip John Schuyler, with whom he had served, gladly used his influence on his behalf, as did several high-ranking judges who had been friends of his father. He was allowed to take the examination, and he passed it brilliantly, the luster of his performance later being dimmed by Alexander Hamilton. Burr studied for ten months, whereas Hamilton, after only six months of study, achieved a grade equally high.

On April 19, 1782, Colonel Aaron Burr, who liked being called by his military title, was admitted to the bar of New York State as a counselor-at-law. He immediately set up an office in Albany, indicating that he also intended to practice in Paramus and that he would move to New York Town when the British evacuated the third largest city in the United States. He thought nothing of working sixteen to eighteen hours a day, and his inheritance having been exhausted by the war, it was not until late June that he was earning enough to support a wife in the style to which Mrs. Prevost was accustomed. She and Aaron were married on July 2, the bride attired in a gown of "suitable gauze," as she wrote to his sister. The bridegroom was scheduled to represent a client in court the following day, so the couple left for Albany by boat a few hours after the wedding.

General Washington sent the newlyweds his best wishes, as did the governors of New York, New Jersey, and Connecticut. Some of the interest shown by persons in high places can be attributed to Theodosia's popularity as a charming hostess, and it can be argued, to be sure, that Washington, who had been given no reason to change his opinion of Burr, was primarily paying a compliment to the bride. The same was not necessarily true of the other highly placed men. After practicing law for slightly less than three months, Burr already represented some of the most influential men in the state, and his brilliance at the bar was attracting notice throughout the country. His family prominence may have called a measure of attention to him initially, it is true, but it was his performance that counted, and many people sensed that he was destined to become a powerful personage in the postwar world.

His marriage was as blissful from the outset as he had promised Theodosia it would be. In spite of the difference in their ages he enjoyed a happiness he had never before known, and he was able to give her contentment, too. Sally Reeve, who visited them for several weeks in the autumn, wrote to her husband that she had never seen such a perfectly matched couple.

Burr's law practice flourished and grew so rapidly that even before the peace treaty officially granting independence to the United States was signed in 1783 and the British formally evacuated New York, he was recognized as one of the state's most prominent lawyers. The assistance rendered by his wife in his swift rise to prominence cannot be overestimated. Already recognized as a leading hostess, Theodosia continued to play that role to the hilt when she and Aaron set up housekeeping together at the Hermitage.

The United States was beginning to emerge from her years of wartime suffering, and a period of dazzling prosperity was beginning. Trade with England was being renewed, trade with France was already assured, and virtually every country in Europe wanted the raw materials that the New World could supply in unlimited quantities. Fortunes were already being made by the shrewd and farsighted, and men were establishing a way of life that their descendants would accept as natural and normal.

It became more and more customary to discuss important business matters at dinner parties, and no one in the environs of New York Town entertained with greater grace than Theodosia Burr, whose dinner invitations were eagerly sought. She and her husband were charming, exceptionally bright, and good conversationalists; her meals were triumphs, and her handsome, dashing husband was already accumulating a wine cellar that would soon be known as one of the country's best.

Visitors not only enjoyed their evenings at the Burr home but were impressed by their confident, self-assured host. When men had legal matters to be attended to, they turned to Aaron Burr, who, it was already said, never lost an important case. It may or may not be true, as Burr boasted in a letter to Matt Ogden, that he had more cases than he could handle and consequently was forced to turn away prospective clients, but the facts speak for themselves. Within one year of opening his first office in Albany Burr was earning as much as any attorney in New York State.

Sir Guy Carleton, the British general charged with bringing the occupation of New York to a close, led his last detachments onto Royal Navy transports on a balmy 1783 day, and the city, occupied for eight long years, reverted to American hands. Aaron and Theodosia Burr were already on hand when the momentous transfer took place. Knowing that real-estate values would rise sharply once the United States assumed jurisdiction, Aaron had anticipated the event by coming down from Albany and renting a house suitable for a rising young attorney and his socially prominent wife.

The large and somewhat pretentious dwelling was located in the best part of town, on Wall Street, only two doors from the city hall and adjacent to the law courts. Making his office in his home, Burr could not have found more convenient quarters.

No man better recognized New York's potential. Boston, the capital of New England, was still the nation's largest metropolis, closely followed by Philadelphia, but Burr felt confident that New York would grow far more rapidly than either of her competitors. Her harbor was America's best, she was a natural center for the trade and commerce of all the states that stretched out along the Atlantic seaboard, and all roads led to her from the West, where a huge spurt in postwar immigration was causing rapid growth.

Displaying the same analytical talents he had shown during the war, Burr now utilized them for his own benefit. Within a decade or two, he felt certain, New York would become the first city of the United States. Therefore, a lawyer who was prominent in New York would almost automatically become a personage of importance everywhere. He and Theodosia could have taken up permanent residence anywhere in the country, but he was so confident of New York's future that he linked his own to it.

In his law practice Burr relied principally on his oratory, his ability to detect weaknesses in the arguments of his opponents, and his shrewd judgment of human nature to win his cases. Unlike such fellow attorneys as John Jay and Alexander Hamilton, he was no great expert in interpreting the law itself. His briefs were sometimes sketchy and on occasion were actually slipshod, but his aggressive, combative nature demanded that he win his cases, and he threw himself into courtroom battles with the same daring, explosive energy he had shown as a soldier.

Within a very short time the people of New York regarded him as the city's first lawyer, a view not shared by many members of the bar, who considered him glib and careless. But Burr was indifferent to their opinion and defined law as "whatever is boldly asserted and plausibly maintained." When it became known that he intended to plead a case, the courtroom was always crowded with spectators, and his audience was so inclined to cheer him that the judges sometimes found it difficult to preserve the decorum of the courtroom essential to dispensing justice.

Serving no master but himself, Aaron was too ambitious to concentrate exclusively on his career as an attorney. He enjoyed luxuries and wanted to live accordingly, so he needed large sums of money for the purpose, and the accumulation of wealth through his practice was too slow and painstaking a process to satisfy him. Certain in his own mind that New York was entering a period of enormous growth, he bought a number of real-estate parcels in the city, hoping he could sell them, within a few years for a handsome profit.

He also began to invest in various land companies that were active in the opening of the West and maintained the financial habit for a number of years. Such investments were highly speculative, in part because many companies did not own clear title to the land they were selling and partly because most companies were flimsy and badly organized.

Aaron Burr was not alone in making such investments. Virtually every prominent citizen of the United States who had cash to spare, and many who could ill afford it, speculated in western land. George Washington put large sums into two such enterprises, banker Robert Morris went bankrupt through such dealings, and Governor Patrick Henry, of Virginia, who was a poor man, borrowed money for the purpose. Even the wealthy John Hancock, who decried the practice, could not resist dabbling in western lands.

In the long run Burr lost more than most because he plunged more consistently and boldly. He was opposed to games of chance, as such, because he thought it stupid to place one's financial hopes on luck rather than reason, but he was merely fooling himself about his land ventures. He would have been shocked, in all probability, had he realized that his speculative investments in the West were a form of gambling. The fact that he never found his pot of gold did not prevent him from spending his money on one attempt after another.

If he lacked the farsighted wisdom of the prudent financial investors, however, he more than made up for it in other realms. His political ambitions were as yet unformed, but he recognized the close alliance of the law and politics and acted accordingly. The city of New York had not been represented in the legislature for years, and when elections were held in the late autumn of 1783 to send men to the Assembly, he ran for a seat. His mounting reputation served him in good stead, making it unnecessary for him to campaign actively, and he won handily over two opponents.

The legislature moved from Albany to New York, which made office-holding a greater convenience for Burr, and from the outset he and Theodosia entertained lavishly. Members of the legislature from other parts of the state were frequent guests, but local political leaders were not forgotten, and they, too, paid frequent visits to the Burr home.

As yet there were no political parties in the true sense. Some men called themselves Whigs, and in the main they were liberal, believed in the rights of the common man, and wanted to invest all powers in the states. The more aristocratic Federalists, currently in the minority, held that only a strong national government could guide the destinies of the United States.

Burr, who had no convictions that would place him in either group, walked a careful tightrope and refused to identify himself as either a Whig or a Federalist. He was the friend and confidant of all fellow politicians, and in the legislature he played the role of a compromiser, thereby winning the affection and trust of both factions. He did favors for everyone, asking nothing in return for himself, but he knew what others did not — that he was building a long-range political bank account and that the day would come when he would demand that the favors be repaid.

Chapter 6

The money poured in endlessly in a steady, golden stream. Burr earned a fee of ten thousand dollars in one case, and in a number of others was paid five thousand. He became so busy that he had to hire several assistants, and he represented the poor only when it served his purposes. Envious colleagues said he had the Midas touch, and it was true that he possessed an extraordinary talent for earning money.

He also spent it as fast as it came in, and sometimes even faster. During the six years from 1783 to 1789 the Burrs lived in three homes, owning rather than renting the last of them, and each was larger and more pretentious than the one before it. Theodosia, whose growing collection of jewels was impressive, rode through the cobbled streets in one of New York's largest carriages. Each year the number of servants on the household staff increased, the new furniture was more expensive, and the wine cellar grew larger.

"Money," Burr said in a letter to his wife, "is contemptible in itself, but truly important and attractive as the means of gratifying those I love."

His relations with Theodosia were unmarred by discord. All five of her children by her previous marriage lived with them, her elder son, John, having resigned his cadetship in the British army, and Burr treated all of them as his own. Within a few years Theodosia's three daughters were married and moved to other parts of the country, so Burr saw them infrequently, but he remained close to both of the boys, John and Frederick, until the end of his life.

During these first six years of marriage Theodosia gave birth to four children, three of whom died in infancy, an indication that the mother herself was not in the best of health, although such deaths were regarded as inevitable in the eighteenth century. The surviving child, a daughter, was given her mother's name and rapidly became her father's favorite.

Little Theodosia inherited Burr's good looks and quick mind and her mother's sweetness of character and charm. Theodosia instructed her in the "womanly virtues," and Aaron taught her to read and write at the age of four and saw to it that she could ride a horse at two. Only his wife's firmness prevented him from giving the child lessons in pistol marksmanship. Their daughter, he told Theodosia, would grow up to possess such intellect, acumen, fortitude, and the ability to stand on her own that she would be the equal of any man — a tall order in an age when women were universally considered to be the inferior sex.

The tutoring of little Theodosia and his stepchildren did not occupy all of Burr's very limited spare time. His own intellectual curiosity was insatiable, and according to his wife, he read an average of three books per week, indiscriminately delving into philosophy, science, economics, and biography. Fortunately he possessed the ability to read very quickly, so the effort did not strain him.

His opportunities to find physical relaxation from his labors had dwindled, and he was forced to attend so many banquets and other functions that they became even more limited. He realized he needed some exercise, however, and set aside thirty minutes of each day for target practice in his yard with his pistols. According to a number of contemporary accounts, he became a deadly shot. Not only could he hit the center of the target on every attempt, but he found it a simple matter to put a bullet through a leaf on a tree or bush, identifying it in advance.

News of his prowess as a marksman spread through New York and on several occasions proved quite valuable. In 1786 he was threatened by the opponents of a client, who informed him, indirectly, that he would be in physical danger unless he dropped the case. Friends urged him to hire bodyguards and to keep his door locked at all times, but Burr disdained their advice.

This was a situation demanding physical courage, and the man who had stormed the gates of Quebec swore he could protect himself. He deliberately left his door unlocked, and he carried two pistols in his belt wherever he went, announcing to the world that anyone who wanted to do him harm was welcome to make the attempt — at his peril.

The men who had threatened him apparently thought better of the idea because no one molested him, and his reputation as a man of valor was enhanced. A few months later a friend asked him if he would have shot to kill had he been attacked, and his answer was as simple as it was direct.

"Of course," he said. "If anyone tries to murder me, I shall dispose of him first."

By 1787 the practice of law had been reduced to a routine and no longer challenged the thirty-one-year-old Aaron Burr. It was still his primary source of income, to be sure, so he took pains never to neglect his work and fought no less hard to gain victories in court. But his real interests were moving in another direction: Government fascinated him because it was a basic source of power. Each of the states was virtually sovereign under the Articles of Confederation, which was the law of the land, and although the national government was assigned certain functions, its acts could be nullified by the legislatures of the states.

Still a member of the New York Assembly, Burr enjoyed his role. He continued to stand apart from partisan politics, however, and refused to take sides in the many quarrels of the day. He was assiduous in protecting the interests of his own constituents, and the Sons of Liberty, the organization of war veterans, knew they could rely on his support whenever they campaigned for land grants, pensions, and other benefits.

Most men were absorbed in the struggle, led nationally by Alexander Hamilton and James Madison, and in New York by Hamilton in person, to change the form of government, adopt a constitution, and strengthen the national executive, legislative, and judicial branches at the expense of the states' powers. The debate raged at length in the New York legislature, where Hamilton, a member, led the fight to adopt the new Constitution, and for many weeks nothing else was discussed. Aaron Burr took no part in the struggle, and while others made impassioned speeches, he sat quietly at his desk, working on documents related to his private law practice.

The arguments for and against the proposed Constitution were exercises in futility, he thought, and confided privately to friends that he did not care which side won. In his opinion the whole question was academic because, he reasoned, neither the Articles of Confederation nor the new Constitution could survive for more than fifty years. Man, he said, was a creature who wanted to be led, so it was probable that within the lifetime of the younger generation the United States would become a monarchy. That development could be avoided only by the establishment of a system that approached it. He suggested that the national chief executive and the members of the upper chamber of a two-part national legislature hold office for life after being elected by the people. The real powers of government would be vested in them, rather than in the lower chamber, whose members would be elected periodically. The governors and other principal administrators of the states would be appointed by the national chief executive, and they, too, would hold office for life.

Inasmuch as all Americans paid lip service to the principles of democracy, Burr knew his own plan had no chance of adoption, so he did not bring it into the open, having no desire to allow his name to become associated with losing causes. It was far better to let events take their natural course.

When it became obvious to him that New York would adopt the new federal Constitution, he ranged himself on the side of the victors and was privately amused when Hamilton praised him for his stand. In another half century at the most, Burr believed, a king would sit on the throne of the United States, so what happened until that time was unimportant. For the sake of public opinion, however, it was preferable that his name be counted in the winners' column.

Soon after the battle over the Constitution subsided, Burr was removed from the political arena of the legislature. Governor George Clinton, elected for his fourth term, asked the energetic young assemblyman to accept appointment to the most important post in his administration, that of Attorney General. For a short time Burr hesitated, realizing his new duties would cut heavily into the time he devoted to his private law practice. Ultimately he accepted, however, because the appointment made him a major figure in the state and enabled him to deal on an equal footing with prominent men elsewhere.

His position also gave him opportunities to augment his income by utilizing his advance knowledge of the location of new roads and bridges, and his real-estate investments increased. He needed additional funds because he and Theodosia had just bought a summer home in Pelham, New York, a handsome estate called the Shrubberies.

In the summer of 1789 the new federal government came to New York to establish its capital there, and Burr was impressed, in spite of his intrinsic beliefs, by its aura of permanence. The new government buildings still under construction were costing a fortune to build, President Washington was treated like a king, and members of the new Congress, particularly those who sat in the Senate, were regarded as majestic figures. The presence of the diplomatic corps enlivened the city's social life, too, and the Burrs were busier than ever before, entertaining and being entertained.

Burr enjoyed the lighter side of the new government, particularly the "spectacle," as he called it, of the fight between the Constitution's two prime movers, Hamilton and Madison, who were interpreting it in different ways. Behind the façade of Aaron's smile, however, his mind was working. The new federal form of government was proving to be far more significant and influential than he had realized it would be, and he made up his mind to rectify his previous error. He intended to stand aside no longer and would become a power on a national scale.

He had his opportunity in early 1791, at the age of thirty-four. Hamilton, whose Federalists controlled the legislature, in 1789 had seen to it that his close associate, Rufus King, and his father-in-law, General Philip Schuyler, won election to the United States Senate. General Schuyler, whose initial term of office ran only two years, confidently expected to be reelected, and it did not occur to him that his post might be contested.

But Burr had set his sights on the seat and knew Schuyler was vulnerable because he was cantankerous, sometimes even autocratic, in his dealings with others. Now was the time, Burr realized, when he could cash in on all the favors he had done for so many in the Assembly over the years.

He waited until Alexander Hamilton, who was serving as Secretary of the Treasury in President Washington's Cabinet, was summoned to Philadelphia on official business. Acting with secrecy and haste, Aaron worked through his friends, saw to it that a special meeting of the legislature was called, and then modestly left the visitors' gallery when he heard himself being nominated for the seat in the Senate.

Federalists who had come to dislike General Schuyler joined forces with the followers of Governor Clinton, and Aaron Burr was elected to the Senate by an overwhelming majority. The old general was rendered speechless by the totally unexpected turn of events.

Secretary Hamilton was no less stunned, and his relations with Senator-elect Burr took a turn for the worse from that time forward. The two had disliked each other from the time they had met during the war, to be sure, but in recent years they had observed the amenities under a truce of sorts. They were the two most prominent lawyers in New York, and in their private practice they had often been teamed together when they represented the same or associated clients. Their wives were friendly, so the Hamiltons went to dinner at the Burr home from time to time, and the Burrs attended various functions at the Hamilton house.

Nothing in the correspondence of either man or, for that matter, of their friends exists to indicate that the surface relationship changed. Both were civilized men, and since Burr was a Federalist, at least theoretically, Hamilton needed all the support for his policies he could muster. But the private correspondence of Alexander Hamilton does reveal that, as he put it, his "eyes were opened at last to the true nature of Burr." In the Secretary's opinion his old acquaintance was a "ruthless adventurer" who would not hesitate to resort to trickery in order to further his own cause.

This view was strengthened at a party given for Burr on the evening of March 3, 1791, the night before he took his seat in the Senate. The guest of honor, in an informal address to his friends, made it clear that he belonged to no political party, that he was beholden to no man, and that he intended to vote as his conscience dictated.

Burr entered the Senate as something of an enigma and relished the speculation that put him in the limelight. He had been in public life for a long time, holding elective and appointive offices over a period of eight years, yet no one knew where he stood on any of the important issues of the day. Although he had delivered hundreds of addresses in the legislature and was one of the most popular banquet speakers in New York, he had made no public utterance on any matter of either domestic or international significance. He had written no letters and talked with no man on anything pertinent to the nation's affairs. In brief, he was an urbane, witty lone wolf, and no one could even guess where he might make his stand.

There were vague rumors that he had materially enriched himself through knowledge he had acquired in his position as Attorney General of New York State, and these stories persisted. Nothing could be proved against him, however, and even his detractors didn't know where to start an investigation of his activities. Some of Hamilton's followers referred to him in their correspondence as the Eel and said he was too slippery to be caught.

By the time Burr took office as a senator, the seat of government had been moved to Philadelphia from New York, and he went alone to be sworn into office, it not being the custom of the day for men to be accompanied by their wives. Besides, even though few people knew it, Theodosia was ailing, her delicate physical condition a never-ending cause of concern to her husband.

He found suitable quarters for himself at 130 South Second Street in Philadelphia and was pleased with them because, as he wrote Theodosia, there was a large yard at the rear of the house where he could find surcease from the troubles of state by indulging in his daily pistol practice. He found himself the immediate target of two strong factions in the Senate from the moment Vice-President John Adams administered the oath of office to him. Political divisions were becoming sharper, in spite of President Washington's strenuous efforts to halt the factionalism that, he feared, might tear the country apart.

The Federalists were united behind Secretary of the Treasury Hamilton, and their opponents were rallying behind the man who, after Benjamin Franklin, was probably the greatest genius of the age — Secretary of State Thomas Jefferson, author of the Declaration of Independence and later destined to serve two terms as President. He and his phalanx called themselves Republicans, the name of their party subsequently being changed to Republican-Democrats and ultimately to Democrats. Relations between the two secretaries were so strained that they spoke only at Cabinet meetings, and there they sparred so viciously that only the good humor of Secretary of War Henry Knox prevented bedlam.

The rupture was already reflected in the Senate, where Federalists sat with Federalists and Republicans went out of their way to avoid the right side of the chamber, joining colleagues of their own persuasion on the left. The new junior senator from New York, it was predicted, would be forced to declare himself when he selected his seat, but Aaron Burr refused to be caught in such an obvious trap.

Senator Rufus King, his New York colleague, presented him, as was the custom; Vice-President Adams administered the oath; and Senator Burr retired to the rear of the chamber. Then, with his colleagues watching him, some openly and some surreptitiously, he moved forward a few feet to the back row, which was appropriate for juniors. His face was solemn as he selected a chair and desk located precisely in the center, neither on the left nor the right. Even John Adams, who was not noted for his sense of humor, laughed aloud at the clever maneuver.

Neither the Federalists nor the Whigs could afford to be offended by Aaron's move, and in the weeks that followed, although both groups courted him assiduously, he smiled at both and aligned himself with neither.

He had written to Theodosia that he expected to lead a lonely life in Philadelphia, but he soon found friends from college and the Continental Army in high government circles. His quarters proved inadequate for the entertaining that had become his custom, so he moved to a more spacious apartment in a rooming house kept by a Mrs. Mary Payne and her widowed daughter, Mrs. Dolley Todd. The fair-haired Dolley was one of the most beautiful young women Burr had ever seen and was as vivacious as she was lovely. She was eager, too, to improve her mind, and he frequently lent her books to read.

Had he not been a married man who loved his wife deeply, Burr might well have become involved in a romance with Dolley. Instead they formed an abiding friendship that lasted through the vicissitudes and disgrace he would suffer in the years ahead. Also, Dolley and the man she later married were in his permanent debt, and neither ever forgot it. James Madison, who had been Aaron's college mate, was his frequent dinner companion, and Burr decided that Madison and Dolley were well matched. He presented his friend to the young lady, then encouraged their romance, and was delighted when they married.

Everyone who knew Aaron Burr believed him to be gregarious and assumed he truly loved the company of others, but there was a streak in his nature of which only Theodosia was aware. It was true that he enjoyed being the center of attention, but constant rounds of social life were wearying, and most people bored him. For a month or two it pleased him to renew old friendships, but thereafter, lonely for his family, he preferred to spend his evenings alone. Mrs. Payne sent his supper to his apartment, and he entertained himself by reading the works of Jean Jacques Rousseau and those of his favorite philosophers.

Burr never missed a session of the Senate during his entire stay there, achieving a perfect attendance record. On the other hand, he introduced no legislation, and although he made a number of addresses, he carefully avoided partisan subjects. His conduct increased the sense of mystery that surrounded him, leading any number of his contemporaries to ask the question, "Why is Aaron Burr a senator?"

The answer was beginning to form in Burr's mind. New ambitions were gripping him, and he was laying long-range plans as audacious as his adolescent dreams of military glory had been.

Chapter 7

Aaron Burr's voting record, attitudes, and approach to various problems were as baffling to Senate-watchers as it was to his colleagues, and his inconsistency made it difficult to categorize him either as a Federalist or as a Republican-Democrat. Occasionally his self-interest could be seen, but his motives in most matters were obscure, and the passage of time has not clarified them.

In some instances he was progressive and farsighted. He was a member of a determined majority who voted in favor of defying the constitutional provision that members of the Senate be native-born, and he fought hard for the admission of the Swiss-born Albert Gallatin, later to become a brilliant Secretary of the Treasury, to the Senate. He was also one of the prime movers of a successful measure to provide Senate galleries for the press and visitors, thus ending the era when the upper chamber met behind closed doors.

On the other hand, he opposed the appointment of his fellow attorney from New York, John Jay, as United States Minister to Great Britain, even though they were well acquainted and had dined together on many occasions. He was far more open in a brief speech he made on foreign affairs, advocating his own appointment as Minister to France as a means of improving and solidifying Franco-American relations.

One of his patterns was consistent, however, as other members of the Senate soon learned. Whenever a vote was scheduled on a highly controversial subject, Senator Burr absented himself from the chamber at the time the tally was taken, even though he kept his attendance record intact by being present during the opening minutes of the session and later reappearing after the voting was completed. It became apparent that he had no intention of permitting foes, active and potential, to pin any labels on the tails of his velvet coat. Amiable in his relations with all of his colleagues, he refused to become involved in disputes, apparently believing that friendship with all was preferable to alignment with a bloc and making efforts to become a leader.

His Senate duties were far from pressing, and he had ample time for other activities. In his college days he had formed the habit of awakening at daybreak so he could have enough time to accomplish all that he wanted to do, and he did not change his ways now. His breakfast was served in his Senate office, and he worked while he ate, directing the activities of a personal assistant and a secretary, who filed documents in metal boxes, which they carefully labeled. By sunrise he had completed his paper work for the day and was free until noon, when the Senate convened.

Never one to waste a moment, he conceived the idea of writing a definitive history of the War of Independence, and for months he worked hard, collecting maps and letters, interviewing others in the government who had been influential in shaping the new nation's affairs in her earliest days, and making a comprehensive outline of the book. As a senator he had access to all records, including secret documents, and he explained to a few friends, Madison among them, that he intended to paint an accurate portrait, even though it might be necessary to portray various heroes of the Revolution in harsh colors.

Word of the project reached President Washington, who had never lost his dislike for the senator from New York and who undoubtedly anticipated the treatment he himself would receive at the hands of the embryo historian. An executive order was issued, and the archives of the government suddenly became inaccessible to Burr. Realizing it would be a waste of time to urge the President to change his mind, he sent an informal appeal to Secretary of State Jefferson, following it with a formal letter. Jefferson's reply was polite, but he said he could do nothing to rescind the order, and the book had to be abandoned. Whether Burr destroyed his outline and notes or whether they subsequently became lost is unknown, but neither in his own lifetime nor later were they found.

The prospect of being idle for several hours each day horrified him, so in 1791 Burr increased his proficiency in foreign languages, learning to speak, read, and write German, Italian, and Swedish and picking up at least the rudiments of Russian. Adding these tongues to the Greek, Latin, French, and Spanish with which he was already familiar, he could claim, with accuracy, that he knew eight languages other than his own.

He also found time to further his own political interests on both national and state levels prior to the 1792 elections. President Washington having consented to accept a second term, it was also believed that Vice-President John Adams would be unopposed for another term. But Burr believed that Adams was not the only man qualified to hold the post, and his friends quietly became active on his behalf in New York, Connecticut, New Jersey, and Pennsylvania. His overall strategy was clear: If he could make a strong showing in those states, Maryland, Delaware, and South Carolina might join his camp. He was willing to concede all of New England except Connecticut to Adams.

Although the campaign was conducted in private, the partisans of Vice-President Adams became alarmed and went to Alexander Hamilton for help. He responded without delay. Also acting quietly, he worked to destroy the base of Burr's strength in New York. He reasoned that if Burr lost support in his home state, his strength would erode elsewhere, and the notion worked out precisely as he planned it. Burr was not too deeply disappointed, as the Vice-Presidency had been a long shot from the outset, but he never forgot or forgave anyone who opposed him and chalked up another grudge against Hamilton.

His hope of becoming Governor of New York seemed to be within his grasp, however, and he used tactics as extraordinary in his own day as they would have been two centuries later. Making no public announcement of his availability, he nevertheless allowed various newspapers in the state to declare him a candidate. Some said he would run as a Federalist, others wrote that he would seek the position on the Republican-Democratic ticket, and a handful said he would run as an independent. All three versions were correct; Burr hoped to snare the support of voters of all three groups.

His clever scheme was doomed when Governor Clinton, who had been thinking of retirement, decided to run for another term as a Republican-Democrat. Alexander Hamilton, the untitled head of the Federalist party in New York, could not ignore the challenges of Clinton and Burr and persuaded the distinguished John Jay to run under the Federalist banner.

Burr could not bear the prospect of defeat, and since he knew he could not win, he withdrew from the race. His bitterness toward Hamilton was evident in a letter he sent Theodosia from Philadelphia.

Then, suddenly, he had a chance to retaliate. Jay won the election, but the votes in several counties were disputed, and the argument was referred to the state's two United States senators. The question was whether a recount of the ballots in those counties should be made.

Senator Rufus King, a staunch Federalist, immediately announced that because no evidence of fraud or other irregularities had been produced, no recount was necessary. Senator Aaron Burr was on a spot. Although he had become expert in avoiding controversial issues, he had no choice in this matter and realized that regardless of what he did, he would antagonize one sector of the electorate. However, his decision was not difficult to make. He had no intention of becoming a Hamilton satellite and knew that the gratitude of the Secretary of the Treasury would be limited. So he cast his vote in favor of a recount.

This deadlock threw the decision into the laps of the New York Board of Electors, which was dominated by the Republican-Democrats. They ordered a recount, and Clinton won reelection. So Aaron Burr stayed in the Senate, his reputation considerably tarnished by his maneuvers. Thomas Jefferson referred to him in his correspondence as a crooked gun. Governor Clinton, who had reason to be grateful, no longer trusted him, and hoping to get him out of active politics, offered him a seat on the Supreme Court of New York, but the offer was declined. Two years later President Washington was blunt in his appraisal when Madison came to him with the suggestion that he appoint Senator Burr as Minister to France. Washington declined, saying he would make no appointment to any office of a man who, in his opinion, lacked integrity.

Tragedy forced Burr's life into a new course in 1794. Late in 1792 Theodosia fell ill, and the efforts of several physicians failed to help her. In the following year her condition was pronounced incurable, and during her husband's absence in

Philadelphia, little Theodosia, the only one of her children still living at home, learned how to prepare doses of laudanum, the strong opiate that killed her pain.

Burr found it impossible to accept the fact that his wife would die and that nothing could be done to save her. He sent an unending stream of physicians to see her, and when each of them concurred in the previous diagnosis, he went on to others. He hired special nurses and attendants, advertised for cures, and even wrote to physicians in London and Paris, requesting all possible help from them. He stayed in Philadelphia only when the Senate was in session, making the long, one-hundred-mile journey home on horseback every weekend, and he gave up all other activities in order to spend every possible moment at Theodosia's side.

Her death in 1794 left him crushed and grief-stricken. It has been said that her passing crippled him emotionally for the rest of his life, allowing him to engage in the nefarious deals that ruined him. She was a woman of honor as well as virtue, and three Presidents of the United States — Washington, Madison, and Monroe — all praised her as one of the great ladies of her era.

Although conjecture is useless, it may he going too far to suggest that Burr would have been a different man had his wife lived. Although her standards were high, she nevertheless had only a limited influence over his activities, and she never took an active interest in politics. Certainly she would have provided their daughter with a greater sense of balance, but it is unlikely that she could have curbed her husband's ambitions or tempered his opportunism. Even if she had been so inclined, and there is no evidence of such a position in the years of their marriage, it is dubious that she would have interfered. Eighteenth-century wives had a well-defined place in the lives of their husbands, and Theodosia was too much of a lady to overstep the mark.

After his wife's death Burr lavished all of his love upon their daughter, the symbol of what he regarded as a perfect union. No matter how busy he might be, he never neglected young Theodosia, spending every available moment with her. He taught her languages, crammed her mind with philosophy and theories of economics, made certain she was an expert horseback rider — and gloried in her growing beauty. She would become the loveliest young woman in the United States, he predicted, and he wanted as much for her as for himself. The little girl reciprocated his devotion, and the pair were close for the rest of their days. Young Theodosia, Burr often declared, was his principal reason for being.

The expiration of his term in the Senate in 1797 sent him into temporary political retirement, but his ambitions were still growing, and he knew now what had to be done to bolster them. His failure to win either the Vice-Presidency or the Governorship of New York five years earlier had been caused, in the main, by his lack of a strong, personal power base, and he was determined to repair that deficiency. A thorough study of affairs in New York had revealed to him precisely what needed to be done, and his instinct was unerring.

The largest of the social organizations in New York City, the fastest-growing metropolis in the country, was a group known as the Tammany Society. Its membership was made up, for the most part, of clerks and artisans, sailors and dockworkers, employees of the new factories that were springing up in the city, and common day laborers. These men gathered on Sundays, holidays, and a variety of special occasions to eat, drink, and engage in athletic trials of strength and skill. The founder of the Tammany Society, William Mooney, conceived the purpose of the club as exclusively fraternal, but the organization's strength ebbed after President Washington inaugurated a campaign, in 1796, against secret societies. Tammany had been open in all of its doings, but the presidential frown caused many members to become inactive.

Tammany was made to order for Aaron Burr's purposes. Its members were ordinary citizens, who, if they voted as a bloc, would gain absolute control of New York City, Semi-moribund and lacking vigorous leadership, it was ready for new blood. Perhaps it was just a coincidence, but Mooney felt neither affection nor respect for Alexander Hamilton and made no secret of his views.

As for Burr, his hatred toward his distinguished colleague was becoming intense. General Schuyler had been returned to the Senate in his place, making him something of a laughingstock, and for a second time Hamilton had moved with firmness and dispatch to deny him the Vice-Presidency, by urging the leaders of the New England and Middle Atlantic states not to consider a candidate he believed to be inferior. So great was Hamilton's power and influence that politicians throughout the country listened to him. Thus there were many scores to be settled.

After meeting with Mooney on several occasions, Burr took over the direction of Tammany's activities but was careful not to join the society himself or to enter its headquarters, called the Wigwam, located near the Battery. He became the mind and heart of the organization, supplying the funds to build its cadres, reorganizing each of the small units that made up its whole, and even giving it a slogan that on the surface was completely lacking in guile. "All men were born free and equal," Tammany declared, quoting Thomas Jefferson.

By late 1797 the society was growing rapidly, new members joining by the hundreds, then by the thousands. The organization's headquarters were moved to larger quarters on Nassau Street, and every Saturday night each member was given a free mug of ale, courtesy of Aaron Burr, to drink to Colonel Burr's health. On July 4, 1798, every Tammany brave was given a four-ounce shot of rum at a mammoth Independence Day celebration, and it was announced that Colonel Burr was responsible for the generous gesture.

Burr's foes viewed the growth of Tammany and his own behind-the-scenes manipulation of the society with ill-concealed alarm. General Schuyler read a speech in the Senate denouncing the use of social clubs for political purposes, and there were many men, within and without the government, who were inclined to suspect that the speech had actually been written by Hamilton, whose style it approached. Hamilton himself was blunt in his own denunciation of the direction in which Tammany was moving, and in his correspondence he denounced Burr as "an embryo of Caesar." The retirement of President Washington to private life and the elevation of John Adams to the Presidency meant that the first citizen of the land was a self-effacing, quiet man, and Hamilton was afraid the young Republic was in danger of disintegration. The two men most to be feared, he declared, were the demagogue Jefferson and the tyrant Burr.

The threat of a war with France in 1798 called a temporary halt to Burr's activities. Washington came out of retirement to become Commander-in-Chief of the Army once again, and General Alexander Hamilton became his deputy. The lore of expanding his military reputation was too great for Burr to resist, and believing that his record entitled him to an appointment as a major general, he hurried to Philadelphia and offered his services to the government. His friends and foes alike were amused to note that he extended himself beyond the amenities of courtesy in an attempt to ingratiate himself with Hamilton.

His efforts were a waste of time, so he turned in another direction and went straight to the top, using all of his charm and powers of persuasion on President Adams. He succeeded so well that his name stood at the top of a list of appointments to the rank of brigadier general, but Hamilton demurred, and Washington's influence was responsible for the removal of his name from the list.

"From all I have known and heard," he wrote to his successor as President, "Colonel Burr is a brave and able officer, but the question is whether or not he has equal talents for intrigue."

Defeated in his new attempt to accumulate fresh military laurels, Burr returned to politics with a vengeance. His control of Tammany was virtually absolute, so his next move was to attempt to capture the rest of the state. He had himself elected to the legislature, once again sitting in Albany. There casting aside his previous caution, he made a number of deliberate moves to win the support of Republican-Democrats everywhere in the state.

He led the attack on the Alien and Sedition Acts passed by the Adams administration as a protective wartime measure, labeling them a threat to the liberties guaranteed by the Bill of Rights. Similarly, he took his stand with Jefferson in his support of the so-called Virginia and Kentucky resolutions, which affirmed the sovereignty of the states. He appealed to the poor by writing and submitting a bill that would abolish debtors' prisons, and he vehemently supported a bill that would have enabled the state's voters rather than members of the legislature to select presidential electors.

The commanding lead of the Federalists in the state was shrinking rapidly, the people were becoming disenchanted with the party, and men everywhere were turning to Aaron Burr, whose fight for what he called the principles upon which the Republic had been founded stirred the hopes and renewed the faith of the disillusioned. They were encouraged, too, by a new institution whose creation had been authorized by the legislature — the Manhattan Bank, which was given the right to print its own specie and granted cash loans in paper money generously and promptly to all deserving Republican-Democrats.

Alexander Hamilton fumed, but there was nothing he could do to halt his opponent's steady accumulation of power and influence. He and a number of others suspected that the philanthropic Aaron Burr was quietly enriching himself through the Manhattan Bank, although nothing could be proved.

A crisis arose in late 1798 when John B. Church, who was Mrs. Hamilton's brother-in-law, voiced his suspicions at a large dinner party. Burr promptly challenged him to a duel, and they met two days later, but Church lost his courage when he went onto the field of honor and faced the country's deadliest pistol shot. He rescinded his remarks and apologized, thereby aborting the duel, and no one else came forward to claim that Aaron was helping himself to money from the Manhattan Bank's till.

Chapter 8

There was little question that Aaron Burr needed money in large quantities. By 1799 his suburban home, Richmond Hill, although a small suburban estate, may have been the most elegant dwelling in New York. His private library numbered between five thousand and six thousand books, most of his furniture had been imported at great expense from England and France, the house was filled with magnificent portraits, statues, and bric-a-brac, and blooded horses occupied every stall in the stables.

The place was the political sanctuary of the state's Republican-Democrats, and such young men as future President Martin Van Buren were frequent visitors. But the estate was far more: Authors and artists, musicians and distinguished teachers, were always welcome, and such men as Washington Irving and John Vanderlyn were pleased to avail themselves of his hospitality. Sophisticates who dined there swore the meals were the finest served in the New World, and Burr's wine cellar had acquired an international reputation. A few, Irving among them, noted that their host himself ate sparingly, never touching rich dishes, and that he confined himself to a single glass of watered wine at a sitting. His food and spirits, it appeared, were served exclusively for the pleasure of others.

He found his own joy in watching the rapid development of Theodosia, now sixteen years of age. She spoke, read, and wrote five languages other than English, and she could hold her own on virtually any subject in conversation with the most renowned guests. She was a beauty with dark-red hair and hazel eyes, and literary guests wrote poems about her supple figure. In winter she skated, during all other seasons she rode, and Washington Irving is the authority for the statement that when she danced, others left the floor so they could enjoy watching her.

Her father's pride in her mind, her appearance, and her accomplishments was limitless. She acted as hostess at Richmond Hill, and a number of suitors began to pay serious court to her. They were discouraged by Burr, however, who made it clear that only the most exceptional of men would be granted permission to marry this most desirable of American girls. He told Theodosia in a letter:

> My property, our home with all of its baubles, mean nothing to me, and whatever honors I have won in this world are empty. You are my only true treasure, and in you is the distillation of all that is pure and noble in your ancestry. Live your life to the full, and beware of giving your heart prematurely, for I will not consent to the gift of your hand to any man who is not worthy of you.

As the turn of the century approached, Burr tightened his grip on Tammany and increased his favors to upstate Republican-Democrats. New York would be the pivotal state in the forthcoming presidential election, and if he could produce a Republican-Democratic victory there, he would be in the position of becoming a kingmaker. The importance of New York did not escape the attention of others, and Alexander Hamilton redoubled his efforts to loosen Burr's grip on the state's voters. Governor Clinton finally having retired, Aaron Burr became the undisputed leader of the Republican-Democratic party, and the most important men of other states began to woo him.

Thomas Jefferson, of Virginia, the national leader of the Republican-Democrats and his party's almost certain candidate for the Presidency, concealed his personal dislike of Burr and sought his friendship. He also utilized the services, as a go-between, of James Madison, his protégé, who was still one of Burr's close friends. The Presidency was a prize worth almost any alliance, and Jefferson did not hesitate to extend his hand to the man he had called, in private, a crooked gun.

As the election of 1800 approached, it became apparent to every politician in the country that Aaron Burr had gained control of the New York electoral-college vote, his Republican-Democrats having won a shattering victory in spite of the efforts of Hamilton and Governor John Jay to halt the tide. Jefferson, writing from his home in Monticello, Virginia, told Madison he considered Colonel Burr a patriot of the first order and asked him to convey the word, in a subtle manner, that if elected President he would appoint the New Yorker to one of "the great offices" at his command.

But Burr felt no particular gratitude and placed no faith in Jefferson's promise. Now forty-four years of age, he had been learning one lesson since the age of nineteen: He had rarely been given a higher rank, even when it had been pledged, and he could put his faith in no one but himself. So he had no intention of accepting Thomas Jefferson's generosity. On the contrary, he decided, he would strike a hard bargain, lending Jefferson his support only if he got what he wanted in return.

His friends conveyed his desires to Albert Gallatin, the head of the Republican-Democratic caucus, which convened in Philadelphia for the purpose of determining the party's national ticket. Although carefully and subtly worded, Burr's message was clear: He would deliver New York to Jefferson but believed his state deserved the Vice-Presidency in return.

The most obvious candidate in the state was George Clinton, the former Governor, who was universally regarded as New York's most eminent Republican-Democrat. Gallatin sent an emissary to Clinton, who agreed to run, and the messenger went to Richmond Hill to confirm the decision. By the time he returned to Philadelphia and reported, however, a significant change had occurred. The name of Clinton was eliminated and that of Colonel Aaron Burr was substituted.

Details of the transactions that occurred at Richmond Hill have remained secret down to the present day. But one thing is certain: Either Aaron Burr or one of his principal aides made it clear that the candidacy of Governor Clinton would not suffice. In return for Burr's support and the delivery of New York's electoral votes, the vice-presidential candidate would have to be Burr himself.

Burr saw what few other men had as yet perceived. His command of the Republican-Democrats in New York was so great that he was moving to the forefront as the party's principal spokesman in all of the northern states except New England, where the Federalists still maintained almost complete control and Republican-Democratic support was negligible. A quiet state-by-state survey told him that with persistence, luck, and some small measure of support in the South, he — rather than Jefferson — might actually be elected President.

The achievement of this coup was possible because of the peculiar nature of the electoral-college vote at that time. The candidate with the largest number of votes became President, and the man who placed second in the balloting became Vice-President. Aaron Burr quietly made up his mind to seek the main prize, but he confided in only a few trusted aides, who were instructed to win support for him wherever possible.

Neither Albert Gallatin nor any of Thomas Jefferson's other friends were aware of what was taking place behind their backs. The caucus, obedient to Burr's wishes, named him as its vice-presidential selection, and everyone concerned believed that Burr would instruct his supporters in the electoral college to yield first place to Jefferson. No one except Burr and his lieutenants knew how high he intended to reach.

The Jefferson camp was surprised but not alarmed when a number of Connecticut electoral-college votes were pledged to Burr. After all, the Burr family was prominent in Connecticut, the one New England state that the Federalists failed to control. Support for Burr also developed in South Carolina, thanks to the work done by some of Burr's associates, but the Jefferson men were still unworried. Their candidate was regarded by many as the nation's most distinguished citizen, and they expected Colonel Burr to instruct some of his supporters to vote for Jefferson, which would enable the Virginian to win the highest office in the land.

Burr, however, had no intention of voluntarily giving up his chance to win the Presidency. He analyzed the situation without sentiment in the late autumn of 1800 and correctly saw that if his bid failed, at the very least he would be elected Vice-President without being beholden in any way to Jefferson. As he saw it — and it was difficult to argue with his conclusion — he had everything to gain and very little to lose by striking out on his own behalf and standing firm.

The electoral-college vote, when it was completed in November, 1800, stunned the entire nation. Thomas Jefferson and Aaron Burr received an equal number of votes and were literally tied for the Presidency!

Some of Jefferson's supporters still expected Burr to yield, and only when he adamantly retained all of the support he had garnered did they understand that he seriously sought the highest office for himself. The tie sent the final disposition of the election to the House of Representatives, where the North was mathematically stronger than the South, and the Jefferson men realized for the first time that their candidate would probably lose.

Members of the Burr camp believed the election of their man was assured, but Aaron failed to share their optimism. While the ordinary people of the country rejoiced because, no matter what the outcome, the Federalists had been defeated, he conducted a careful head count and knew his foes would have the last word. Since neither he nor Jefferson could command a Republican-Democratic majority in the House, the votes of Federalist representatives would decide the Presidency.

Hectic maneuvering occupied the last days of 1800 and the first weeks of 1801. The northern Federalists in the House united behind President John Adams, but the South had its own Federalist candidate, Charles C. Pickney, of South Carolina, and tired of the party's domination by New England and New York, it refused to yield. The outcome of the election was anyone's guess.

The House gathered on February 11, 1801, to decide the issue, with the Senate members acting as monitors. Vice-President Jefferson, the presiding officer of the Senate, automatically had the disagreeable task of counting the ballots and in order to ward off future protests, assigned senators friendly to other candidates to help him.

The tally produced another stunning surprise. Jefferson and Burr were still tied for the lead, with each receiving seventy-five votes; Adams received sixty-five, sixty-four were cast for Pickney, and John Jay received one. Had the supporters of

Adams and Pickney been able to unite behind one or the other, that candidate could have won.

The situation was so tense that the House decided to cast its next ballot in secret, with only members of the Senate as witnesses. The press and visitors' galleries were closed, and a deeply embarrassed Thomas Jefferson retired to his lodgings, thankful that his presence was no longer required.

The close vote created havoc throughout the nation. In New England the states mustered their militia, the Federalists spoke of secession from the Union, and it was commonly assumed that the regiments being mustered would fight for the creation of a separate nation. New York, Pennsylvania, and New Jersey, supported by Connecticut and Delaware, remained firmly entrenched in Aaron Burr's camp, whereas the South and West were divided, some favoring Jefferson, others demanding Pickney. Bonfires burned in scores of cities and towns, and bands of men and youths roamed through the streets, shouting slogans and demanding the appearance of their foes.

Alexander Hamilton viewed the situation with dismay. Either Thomas Jefferson or Aaron Burr would become the next President, and he placed no faith in either man. Even more frightening was the possibility that unless the issue was settled with dispatch, there might be no united nation to govern. People everywhere were so aroused that the entire nation threatened to disintegrate. In Connecticut civil war was expected to erupt at any moment, since Hartford, the largest town, was the Federalist capital, and the rest of the state was in Burr's Republican-Democratic camp.

The House, in its wisdom, decided to limit the candidacy to the two leaders — Jefferson and Burr — and to vote by states, each state's members holding their own caucus and casting a single ballot. There were sixteen states then in the Union, so the vote of nine would be required to give the winner a majority. On the first ballot taken under this system, Jefferson received eight votes, six were cast for Burr, and in two states the delegates split precisely, creating ties that nullified their votes.

Jefferson was in the lead, but it appeared that Aaron Burr would win, largely because the Federalists, who now held the balance of power, believed he would prove more reasonable than his opponent and hence would be more likely to accept their approach to many problems. So most of them continued to cast their votes for Burr, and the deadlock continued. After thirty-five ballots, which lasted all through the week and into the next, there was no change.

Then, at last, Alexander Hamilton intervened. In his opinion Jefferson was the less evil of the contenders, and although unable to agree with almost any of the Virginian's views, he knew that the distinguished Vice-President was a man of integrity. He could not say the same of Aaron Burr and told the Federalists that he considered his fellow New Yorker the "Cataline of America."

Hamilton devised a strategy to meet the situation, urging the Federalist members of some state delegations to refrain from voting or casting blank ballots, which would enable the Republican-Democrats committed to Jefferson to carry those states. These members of the House accepted his advice, and on the thirty-sixth ballot Thomas Jefferson became the third President of the United States. Aaron Burr automatically became Vice-President.

The election, the strangest in American history, caused a number of sharp repercussions. Prior to the next election the ratification of the Twelfth Amendment to the Constitution prevented a repetition of such a situation in the future by providing that balloting for President and Vice-President be separated. The 1801 crisis also marked the decline and almost total eclipse of the Federalist party, which shriveled and vanished everywhere except in New England.

The bizarre events of the winter also had a marked influence on the newly elected Vice-President of the United States. Burr had maintained a serene surface decorum throughout the crisis, remaining at his Richmond Hill estate and giving the appearance of keeping his hands off. Jefferson, on the other hand, had stayed in Philadelphia and had gone daily to his office, leading some members of the Burr camp to charge that he had tried to influence the members of the House. But appearances had been deceptive, and everyone in touch with the situation knew it.

The truth of the matter was that the Burr followers had done everything in their power to persuade — and in a few instances even to force — various representatives to change their votes in favor of their candidate. Jefferson, on the other hand, had been scrupulous in his refusal to use influence on any individual member of the House.

The true facts, combined with Aaron Burr's pious pose, alienated many who had supported him, and on reflection they were relieved that Jefferson had been elected. In addition, it was well known that Burr had forced himself into the running when it had been taken for granted that Jefferson would be the candidate of the Republican-Democrats. His refusal to abide by the decision of the party leader's caucus made him far more foes than friends. President Jefferson obviously considered him untrustworthy, an attitude that was reflected by most men in high places.

Had Burr exercised patience, had he seen to it that New York's electoral-college votes were cast for Jefferson in accordance with the original plan, he would have stood first in line for the Presidency when Jefferson retired. A tradition had already been created: Vice-President Adams had succeeded President Washington, and now Vice-President Jefferson had succeeded President Adams. It would have been natural for Vice-President Burr to succeed President Jefferson.

But Burr was already paving the way for his downfall. One of his greatest character faults was his impatience, and he had been so eager to seize the Presidency that honorable men were shunning him.

Even more significant was the rupture of his relationship with Alexander Hamilton. Ever since the early days of the war, or so it seemed, Hamilton had stood in his path, blocking his advancement at critical junctures. Now, because of Hamilton's intervention, Burr had been denied the highest office in the country.

Hamilton was his enemy, and when their paths crossed again, Burr was determined not to emerge the loser.

Chapter 9

The Constitution of the United States specifies only one responsibility for the Vice-President, that of presiding over the Senate, and Vice-President Aaron Burr had literally no other function to perform. President Jefferson, who treated him with a cool, almost detached reserve, not only held him at arm's length, but gave him no place in the councils of the administration. Many others — in the Cabinet, the Senate, and the House — followed the President's example, and Burr became something of a social leper in Philadelphia.

A few old friends, among them Secretary of State James Madison and his wife, continued to see him, but he was forced, in the main, to rely exclusively on his own company except on those occasions when one of his New York cronies paid a brief visit to the capital.

The situation was ironic in the extreme, a fact no one appreciated more than Burr himself. The Vice-Presidency was a post of distinction, but the man who held that place of honor was treated by others in the government as an outsider unworthy of their notice. This, he believed, was caused by the simple fact that he had refused to play the role of a hypocrite and had tried to advance his own ambitions rather than another's.

He brooded over the injustice that had been done to him, but he was also still feeling the depressing effects of a recent personal crisis — the unexpected romance of his daughter — to which he had been forced to acquiesce despite his own negative feelings. One of young Theodosia's frequent companions since, early adolescence had been Joseph Alston, a

South Carolinian, now twenty-one years of age. A member of a wealthy Charleston family, he had spent his summers with relatives who owned a home on the Hudson River in New York and had been a member of a group of youngsters with whom Theodosia, almost four years his junior, had gone riding and swimming.

It was Alston's family connections that had placed South Carolina in the Burr camp for a time during the recent elections, and Aaron was duly grateful for the influence that had been exerted on his behalf. However, the price he was being asked to pay was too great for him to tolerate. Alston was anything but the husband for whom he had been grooming his beloved daughter. The young man was handsome, and his manners were impeccable, but although he could speak French and Spanish, his knowledge of languages was far inferior to Theodosia's; in no way was he her intellectual equal. More serious than any of these considerations, however, was his total lack of ambition. His family's wealth made it unnecessary for him to work, so he had no intention of earning a living. His interest in politics was almost nonexistent, even though he had the opportunity, if he chose to exert himself, to become one of the most powerful men in his state.

Theodosia, whose command of logic was usually awe-inspiring, failed to see the faults in Alston that her father found. Casting aside the exercise of reason that had guided her since early childhood, she fell in love with her suitor. Burr's disappointment was bitter, but he could not deny Theodosia anything she desperately wished, so he reluctantly consented when Alston requested permission to pay formal court to her.

For a short time Theodosia exercised her prerogative and demonstrated the inconsistency of a young girl by refusing to accept Alston's repeated proposals of marriage, but she soon abandoned her pose of independence and capitulated.

The wedding was held at Richmond Hill in late February, 1801, before her father actually became Vice-President of the United States, and was a mammoth affair. Everyone to whom Aaron was politically indebted was invited. Most of the leaders of the Tammany Society were in attendance, as were the upstate faithful with whom he was continuing to maintain ties.

Burr put on a brave front and played the role of father of the bride to the hilt, but he was deeply concerned. Even Theodosia's friends were surprised by the choice she had made, and several of these young women confided to him that they thought Alston was dissipated, ill-tempered, vain, and silly. At the huge reception that followed the marriage ceremony he quietly told several of his cronies that his dueling pistols would be put to good use if Alston dared to abuse the precious Theodosia.

The bride and groom departed a few hours after the reception, and the following day a lonely Aaron Burr went off to Washington City, the nation's new capital. His mood already low, he could have gone off to no more dreary a place. Created by an act of Congress, the embryo community was located adjacent to the swamps of the Potomac River, standing between Virginia and Maryland, and by no stretch of anyone's imagination was it yet a city.

There were two cores — the President's House, as yet unpainted, and the drafty Capitol, which stood on a hill. They were connected by a rutted dirt road named Pennsylvania Avenue, which bore the distinction of being the only completely cleared thoroughfare in town. A number of government buildings were still under construction, as were private homes and lodging houses, and the sounds of saws and hammers could be heard day and night. So few facilities were available that government officials were unable to bring their wives and children with them. No foreign legations had been constructed as yet, so members of the diplomatic corps, like senators and Cabinet members, were obliged to take refuge in rooming houses.

Meals were served to the residents of these hastily constructed dwellings, because as yet there were no taverns, inns, or other eating places in the immediate area; the nearest were located in Alexandria, Virginia, a two-hour ride on horseback. There were no distractions in the town, the food was inferior, and the rooming houses stocked no wine. No laundresses, tailors, or others who provided services for the gentry had put in an appearance. The town was as primitive as a frontier community located in the wilderness of Kentucky or Tennessee.

Thomas Jefferson set the tone of his administration by walking the length of Pennsylvania Avenue to his inauguration, spattering mud on his boots and trousers. Burr, along with everyone else, was forced to follow the same procedure, and he later complained that the new President's display of false modesty had ruined a new suit he was wearing for the first time. The new President and Vice-President took the oath of office from Chief Justice John Marshall, himself recently appointed, and he, too, was mud-smeared.

Theodosia and her husband journeyed to Washington City from South Carolina for the inauguration, arranging to stay with friends in Virginia. That evening they accompanied Burr to the President's House for Jefferson's informal reception and then went off to Virginia, leaving Aaron alone. An invisible wall separated him from the other guests, and although no one said or did anything untoward, he felt so uncomfortable that he returned early to his cramped quarters in a nearby rooming house. While other members of the new administration celebrated the day of the ordinary citizen with drink and song, the new Vice-President retired to his bed.

Burr soon learned he would play no active role in the new administration. He was not invited to attend Cabinet meetings, and neither the President nor anyone else explained plans or policies to him. On the first Tuesday of each month he attended the informal dinners that President Jefferson gave for all senior members of the administration, but at no other time was he invited there. On these occasions no one ever sought his counsel, and he learned to keep silent and remain in the background, a difficult task for a man who habitually enjoyed dominating a conversation.

Only in his official duties as Vice-President did he emerge from the shadows. Faithful in his Senate attendance, he presided impartially, and although he was strict in his observance of parliamentary procedures, his wit was a leavening influence. Even the most adamant of his foes were forced to admit that he was the best presiding officer the Senate had yet known.

When Congress adjourned, Aaron Burr hurried off to New York, using his influence over the Tammany Society to win George Clinton a sixth term as Governor. Thereafter he presided with éclat over a convention called to change the state's constitution. If he expected George Clinton's friendship or gratitude for his help in winning New York's chief executive another term, he was disappointed; the Governor treated him with the same distant, polite attitude President Jefferson displayed.

Burr was indifferent to the personal opinion of both men, but he was hurt by their bland refusal to grant him the patronage he believed he deserved. Tammany continued to support him, as did a handful of the upstate faithful, which was gratifying, but he realized he would have to distribute a number of federal and state jobs if he hoped to command their continuing allegiance. Neither were forthcoming. Governor Clinton ignored his recommendations, and not one man Burr named was given a state position, even though Tammany was responsible for the Governor's reelection.

Jefferson's disregard of Burr's wishes was even more blatant. The Vice-President sent a brief letter to the President, urging that a number of "highly qualified" men whom he named receive various government appointments. Jefferson refused to give a post to any of them and seemed to go out of his way to embarrass Burr. Robert Livingston, one of the few New Yorkers who had been in Jefferson's camp from the outset, was offered the Navy Department, and when he declined it, the President made him Minister to France. Livingston's brother, Edward, became United States District Attorney for New York, and thereafter all patronage in the state was channeled through him rather than through the Vice-President.

Inasmuch as no rules, formal or otherwise, governed the award of government posts, Burr had no legitimate protest. He could only nurse his grievance in private while he watched even Tammany's support crumble away. He had good cause to believe that his enemies, among whom President Jefferson and Governor Clinton stood high on the list, were not content to humiliate him, but were intent on driving him out of politics and sending him, impotent and broken, back to private life.

He moved cautiously and slowly to determine the nature and intent of the opposition. The failure of the President to act on his recommendation that a minor federal post in New York be given to one of his aides, Matthew Davis, of the Tammany

Society, gave him the chance to scout the enemy. He sent a letter to Secretary of the Treasury Albert Gallatin, who was still head of the Republican-Democratic caucus, and said in part:

> Strange reports are here in circulation respecting secret machinations against Davis. The arrangements having been made public by E. L. [Edward Livingston], the character of Mr. D. is, in some measure, at stake on the event He has already waived a very lucrative employment in expectation of this appointment, and Davis is too important to be trifled with.
>
> If you will show to the President what above relates to this appointment, you will save me the trouble of writing and him that of reading a longer letter to him on the subject.

The communication put Gallatin on the spot. He had no liking for Aaron Burr and had good reason to mistrust him but thought it would be a mistake for the administration to go out of its way to antagonize him. Three years remained before the next presidential election, and a great deal could happen-during that time, but the Vice-President had already demonstrated that his capacity for troublemaking was enormous. It would be wise, Gallatin thought, to win Burr's cooperation and help, and if that goal was unattainable, every effort should at least be made to neutralize him.

The Secretary not only discussed the matter with President Jefferson, showing him Burr's letter, but went a step farther and wrote a formal communication of his own, recommending the nomination of Davis. He explained his reasons in a covering letter: New York would be a pivotal state in the election of 1804, just as it had been in 1800, and it was far from certain that it would be in the Republican-Democrat camp. The President's most prominent and implacable political foe, Alexander Hamilton, who had been retired to private life, would do everything in his power to prevent the reelection of Jefferson. It was possible, even probable, that the Federalists might try to revive their party by making Burr their candidate. Hamilton and Burr, standing together, possessed an unlimited joint talent for creating mischief, and they had to be neutralized.

Gallatin's arguments were so persuasive that Jefferson finally consented to see Davis and then make up his own mind in the matter. The Tammany chieftain was summoned to Washington City, and in a private interview with the President he made the mistake of singing Aaron Burr's praises as, out of loyalty, he tried to convince the Chief Executive that the Vice-President was the worthiest of Americans.

Davis failed to win the appointment. Precisely as Gallatin had predicted, Burr interpreted the rejection as a hostile act directed at him and quietly declared war on the Republican-Democrats in general and President Jefferson in particular. Before long he was verbally handcuffing the President's supporters in Senate debates, cutting short their speeches, denying them the floor, and otherwise disrupting their activities. He always acted within the strict framework of parliamentary procedure, however, and his sense of humor was so sharp that he made it plain he intended no personal slight against the speaker.

The strain in the relations between the President and Vice-President became so great that late in the autumn of 1802 Burr politely declined an invitation to the regular monthly dinner with members of the administration. He made no secret of his feelings, however, and when someone tactlessly asked why he had missed the dinner, he is supposed to have replied, "I had no wish to be a killjoy, and knew that my presence would have overpowered the company."

In due course the comment was repeated to the President, and Jefferson did not extend another invitation. The two men rarely met after that, and other members of the administration began to avoid the Vice-President at all times.

In the winter of 1802-1803 Aaron Burr made a significant change in his Washington City style of living. By this time the town had doubled in size and boasted several hotels and taverns, as well as large, comfortable rooming houses. He engaged a spacious suite in one of the latter, brought in quantities of his own furniture, and generally put the place in shape for the entertainment of his own guests. The Republican-Democrats might regard him as anathema, but they weren't the only people who lived in Washington City. A number of Federalists and ex-Federalists were there, along with many others who had no use for Thomas Jefferson, his followers, or the principles of advancing the cause of the ordinary citizen.

A growing diplomatic colony was also thriving in Washington City by this time. It was the duty of the ministers and their assistants to cultivate the President and Secretary of State, which they did, inasmuch as Jefferson and Madison were two of the most cultured men in the community, the task imposed no hardship on them. They found a majority of the rough-hewn Republican-Democrats difficult to accept, however, and sought social relief elsewhere.

They found it in the company of the urbane Vice-President. Burr had his own kitchen installed in his suite and transferred some of his fabulous stock of wines from the cellar at Richmond Hill to his Washington City abode. His dinner parties were civilized affairs reminiscent of similar dinners given in the capitals of Europe. The food was delicious, the wines were first-rate, and the conversation, which never touched on American politics, was witty and sophisticated. No diplomat rejected an invitation to dine with Vice-President Burr.

So it transpired, probably not by accident, that Burr was soon on the friendliest of personal terms with Don Carlos Martinez de Yrujo (the Marquis de Casa Yrujo), Spain's Minister to the United States, and Anthony Merry, Britain's Minister to the United States. Both were destined to play major roles in the drama that would destroy Burr's future and win him the contempt of his fellow Americans.

Chapter 10

By the end of 1802 Aaron Burr was in financial difficulties. He received a salary of five thousand dollars per year as Vice-President, a sum that barely paid for his lodgings and entertainments in Washington City. He made frequent visits to Theodosia and her husband in South Carolina, he kept a large stable of horses, and the expenses of maintaining Richmond Hill were considerable. So he had to dip into previous savings in order to live in the style to which he had accustomed himself. Meanwhile, the business community had little confidence in the Jefferson administration, a number of companies were bankrupted, and some of Burr's investments soured. He was forced to borrow a substantial sum from his son-in-law and then turned to the New York moneylenders for additional cash.

Life at Richmond Hill had lost its savor without the presence of Theodosia, so he decided to dispose of the estate, hoping to realize enough to pay off his debts. He asked the staggering sum of $150,000 for the property and contents of the house, the equivalent of about $600,000 a century and a half later. Richmond Hill well may have been worth the price he set, but very few men in the new, struggling United States could afford to pay that much for a home, and a number of potential buyers were frightened away. The end result was that he was forced to keep the estate, and his financial problems multiplied.

In the political arena the entire country watched every move he made. It was common knowledge that he had become a virtual outcast from the inner circles of government, and additional interest stemmed from the fact that he had abandoned his party a little more than a year after taking the office of Vice-President. Former Federalists everywhere began to take heart, but Alexander Hamilton failed to confer his blessings on one who might have taken shelter in the upper echelons of the Federalist hierarchy, so Aaron Burr continued to stand alone.

In the autumn of 1802 he received the only news that cheered him. Theodosia Burr Alston intended to make a contribution to the growing population of South Carolina in the spring. Burr immediately began sending reams of instructions to his daughter and son-in-law, prescribing Theodosia's diet, telling her how, when, and how long to exercise, and generally making a nuisance of himself. He demanded and received reports on his daughter's health from the physician in charge of her case, and he fretted endlessly because the reports were too short.

Theodosia and her husband managed to remain calm and sensible in spite of his excitement, and the following May Aaron Burr Alston came into the world, to the delight of his grandfather, who gave a large dinner party in his honor.

"One would think," Dolley Madison observed, "that no man before Aaron ever had a grandson. He expands so much at the mention of the child that I live in dread, afraid he will burst."

The arrival of Theodosia's baby, more than any other single factor, caused Aaron Burr to ponder long and hard the subject of his future. As of the late spring of 1803 he had only a debt-riddled estate and a clouded name to leave to his grandson and namesake. The time had come for him to rehabilitate himself and restore his fortunes.

Money, as such, still meant nothing to him, perhaps because he knew he could earn vast sums if he chose to return to private life and resume his New York City law practice. His familiarity with everyone who held high government office and with scores of other influential politicians throughout the country would be a help to him in that practice, and it was no secret that he and Chief Justice Marshall, who had been one of Virginia's leading Federalists prior to his judicial appointment, addressed each other by their first names.

The private practice of law, however, neither challenged nor interested Aaron Burr. He had missed election to the Presidency by a hair, he had become immersed in the political scene, and like so many men in high places who have followed him in American history, he was mesmerized by the power that federal officialdom exerted. Having tasted that power and craving more, he had no appetite for anything else.

In the summer of 1803 his friends in the Tammany Society tested the political waters on his behalf and found them chilly. Neither the Republican-Democrats nor the remnants of the Federalist party were interested in giving high office to the unreliable Aaron Burr. Members of both groups were uneasy over the prospect of his active return to the arena, and at a New York dinner party one of Hamilton's lieutenants repeated what was alleged to be his superior's observation to the effect that Mr. Burr had intrigued to gain the Presidency and having failed, was intriguing again. The comment found its way into print in a political pamphlet.

Aaron Burr, consciously or otherwise seeking revenge, felt his honor had been impugned and announced his intention of challenging Alexander Hamilton to a duel. Before he could arrange to have seconds call on Hamilton, however, he received a letter of apology from his former colleague. This gesture was followed by a statement Hamilton made to the New York *Post*, in which he denied knowledge of any intrigue on Burr's part to obtain the Presidency.

This clever gesture did more than rob Burr of the excuse to fight a duel. Thousands of people who had not seen the little pamphlet in which the charge first appeared read Hamilton's remarks in the *Post*. This was the first they had heard of any supposed intrigues, and they began to wonder about the matter, linking it in their minds with Aaron's departure from the ranks of the Republican-Democrats. In a single, deft move Hamilton had succeeded in undermining the confidence of New York City's citizens in the man who was still their undisputed political leader.

Early in 1803 the first cracks of sunlight appeared in the gloom. One of Edward Livingston's assistants absconded with large sums of government money, and the deeply embarrassed Livingston covered the shortage with his own funds, resigned his office, and left New York to take up residence in New Orleans. Newspapers favorable to Burr crowed in triumph, while President Jefferson maintained complete silence.

But Aaron Burr's joy was short-lived. Robert Livingston, the Minister to France, had discovered that the Emperor Napoleon I, whose interests lay in Europe and who found it difficult to maintain communications with overseas possessions, might be willing to sell the vast Louisiana Territory to the United States. James Monroe was sent to Paris as a special envoy to help in the secret negotiations with French Foreign Minister Charles Maurice de Talleyrand-Perigord.

On April 30, 1803, an astonishing treaty was signed in Paris. In return for the relatively small sum of eighty million francs, the entire Louisiana Territory was ceded to the United States, which more than doubled her total land area, gained control of the Mississippi River, and stretched halfway across the North American continent. Signatures scribbled on a sheet of paper transformed the weak, young Atlantic seaboard nation into a potential power of the first rank, the largest and most important in the New World.

When they learned the news a month later, most American citizens were delighted, but a minority expressed some misgivings about the transaction. New Englanders were afraid their part of the country would decline in influence and importance, and some New Yorkers shared that sentiment. A vocal handful in the West wanted to continue the sweep toward the far Pacific, taking territory from Spain.

Aaron Burr accepted the news of the acquisition of the Louisiana Territory with seeming calm, but he knew, as did most expert politicians, that no man could defeat Thomas Jefferson for reelection the following year. The President's popularity had soared to such heights that it would be impossible for anyone to overcome his lead.

So an ambitious man in the prime of life at the age of forty-seven was forced to think of his own future in new terms. It was in 1803 that Aaron Burr actually began to engage in the intricate intrigues that would lead to his ruin. A master plan was developed in that year in which he was supposed to play the leading role, but on one, down to the present day, has been able to discover how much of the basic idea can be attributed to him or who evolved it with him. His voluminous correspondence was penned in a number of complicated codes, and each of his many correspondents kept in touch through the medium of a separate and distinct code. Historians have been unable to unravel the mystery, in part because so many letters have been lost to posterity and partly because so many of the codes have proved indecipherable.

According to this scheme, Aaron Burr would run for the Governorship of New York in the spring of 1804. The rest of the plan depended upon his success at the polls. He was the only man strong enough, he and his fellow intriguers reasoned, to lead New York out of the Union in a joint move with the New England states, which would secede at the same time. Together these states would form a new, independent nation, and inasmuch as they controlled most of the manufacturing and commerce of North America, the truncated United States would be forced to recognize and deal with them. As the leader of the secession movement Aaron Burr would be made President of this new nation.

There was an alternative open to Burr, to be sure, and he decided to explore it before advancing his plot. The task of administering the huge Louisiana Territory was enormous, and few men were qualified to act simultaneously as a civilian governor and a military governor. Burr considered himself one of the few. He sent several feelers in the direction of the President's House, but there were no replies, so he made an appointment with Jefferson.

The two men met in an atmosphere of cautious, strained cordiality, and for a time they talked in circles. At last Burr broached the subject of the Governorship of the Louisiana Territory, making it plain that his friends in New York would win New York for the President when Jefferson stood for reelection the following year.

Thomas Jefferson was tempted. He felt he had no need of Burr's help, but it would be a great relief if the country's most active troublemaker were living in far-off New Orleans, acting as his country's viceroy. But there were aspects of the situation that caused the President to hesitate. He knew militiamen were drilling in New England for some unexplained purpose, and he had picked up enough scraps of information to form a vague idea of the Burr plot. He was also convinced that Burr, living and working hundreds of miles from the Atlantic seaboard, would be beyond the control of the government. As civilian-military Governor of the Louisiana Territory he would become a law unto himself, and it was possible he might try to carve a new nation for himself in the West.

Unwilling to take the risks, Jefferson retreated to the position he had taken in 1800: He would make deals with no one in order to ensure his reelection.

Rebounding from the President's summary rejection of his proposal, Burr quickly announced that he intended to seek the Governorship of New York as an independent Republican-Democrat. Governor Clinton and Robert Livingston, now his close associate, would be certain to name a candidate on the regular Republican-Democratic ticket. What the Federalists would do was in doubt, but Burr and his lieutenants hoped their hatred for Jefferson was so great they would nominate no candidate of their own but would give him their support.

Even if the Federalists surprised him by putting a candidate in the field, however, he felt certain he would win. The renewed support of Tammany virtually guaranteed that he would carry New York City, where the largest number of the state's citizens lived, and the other two candidates would split the upstate vote, thereby enabling him to sweep into office.

Abandoning the dull routines of Washington City after making some highly secret arrangements there that were known to no other American, he returned to Richmond Hill to take personal charge of his campaign. While he was there, he also held a number of private meetings with Roger Griswold, a representative of the New England Federalists, to whom he gave solemn assurances that the new republic he and the Federalists would establish together would be completely democratic and that the personal liberties of all men would be guaranteed by a constitution.

This election, of all the races in which Aaron Burr had participated, was one he felt compelled to win. So much more than met the ordinary citizen's eye was at stake. Actually, his whole future — as well as that of the grandson who bore his name — hung in the balance in the daring enterprise he and his friends had conceived. Working indefatigably, he made every effort to insure that no phase of the campaign was neglected, and he labored in person to win the support of the state's Federalists.

He appeared to be successful. The Federalists held an unannounced meeting in Albany, and Burr was privately informed that the group would second the nomination made by his own independent Republican-Democrats.

But Burr failed to consider the possible intervention of Alexander Hamilton, who had supposedly retired from the active political arena after the election of Jefferson as President in 1801. Hamilton had heard rumors of the grand scheme being concocted by Burr and the New England Federalists, and whether he gave them credence or rejected them as absurd is beside the point. He placed no faith in Aaron Burr and was afraid the Union he had worked so hard to create would be in danger if such a man became the chief executive of New York.

Accordingly, he traveled to Albany, appeared uninvited at the meeting of the Federalists, and before they voted to second the nomination of Burr, made a long, impassioned speech urging his fellow colleagues not to take such a step. No record of the address was preserved, but it served its purpose at the time. The Federalists listened, stared at each other when Hamilton stalked out of the room after completing his speech, and then voted unanimously not to endorse the Burr candidacy.

Thereafter, the confusion was so great that they did not support anyone.

The Federalist flurry supposedly took place in private, and no details were printed by the newspapers, but the whole story was repeated to Burr. According to the accounts of several close associates, he lost his well-controlled temper for the first time in years and cursed Hamilton viciously. He was not surprised to learn, however, that his foe was writing letters to many men of substance, urging them to campaign actively against the Vice-President, and that he hammered at the same theme at dinner parties and other functions.

A month prior to the election the Burr-controlled press moved into high gear. The New York *Chronicle*, which had been established with funds supplied by Aaron when he had controlled the destinies of the Manhattan Bank, published a series of outright falsehoods, claiming that both President Jefferson and Alexander Hamilton were giving Burr their unqualified support. Other newspapers promptly branded the allegations as lies, and Hamilton was prompted to issue a statement in which he flatly denied that he favored the election of the man he mistrusted.

Just prior to the state election the national Republican-Democratic caucus held a significant meeting and after endorsing President Jefferson for another term, named George Clinton as its choice for Vice-President. This rebuff to the incumbent did Burr no good and may have been responsible, in part, for his overwhelming defeat by Morgan Lewis. Never before had a candidate for the Governorship of New York lost by such an overwhelming margin.

It was obvious to Burr as it was to everyone else that his political career, on both national and state levels, had come to an end. Republican-Democrats and independent voters wanted nothing to do with him, the remnants of the Federalist party rebuffed him, and Tammany, having learned there was no profit in supporting a loser, also turned away from him.

On the surface Burr accepted his fall with good-humored grace. Even in his letters to his daughter his attitude appeared to be one of philosophical resignation, but in private he was seething, and as subsequent events demonstrated, he was determined to force a personal showdown with Alexander Hamilton, his nemesis for more than a quarter of a century.

Chapter 11

As nearly as posterity can judge, Aaron Burr cannily awaited the right opportunity — some might call it the excuse — to challenge Alexander Hamilton to a duel. His chance came on June 18, 1804, when he learned that Hamilton allegedly had made "despicable" references to him in a conversation with mutual acquaintances. One of his still-faithful aides, Billy Van Ness, paid a call on Hamilton, who appeared surprised and said he did not recall any such conversation.

Burr immediately entered into a correspondence with his old enemy, charging him, in a bristling letter, with being evasive. Hamilton tried to soothe his ruffled feathers in a diplomatic reply, but Burr refused to be mollified, and his next letter was even more hostile. As the exchanges continued, it became evident that he was intent on forcing the issue, and Hamilton finally reached a point from which he could no longer retreat with dignity and honor. He had succeeded Washington as Commander-in-Chief of the Army, a post he still held, and he felt he would appear craven in the eyes of his subordinates if he continued to evade a fight.

He accepted the challenge.

Burr, as the supposedly injured party, had the choice of weapons and elected to fight with pistols. Hamilton, like everyone else who knew Aaron Burr, realized there was no more expert marksman in the country.

The engagement was delayed for the better part of two weeks while Hamilton attended to some unfinished legal business, and in public, at least, he gave no sign of the trepidation he felt. Only later was it revealed, in his new will and a letter to his wife, that he felt certain he would be killed.

During the period prior to the duel Burr spent long hours on the target range at Richmond Hill. It was common knowledge that he appeared there after an early breakfast each day and remained until noon, firing pistol after pistol at a crudely drawn sketch of a man drawn on a block of thick wood. When that target splintered, he used a second, then a third.

The two antagonists met by accident at an Independence Day banquet on July 4, and although they did not shake hands, they exchanged seemingly amiable words. Several mutual acquaintances tried to patch up their differences, but the effort failed; Burr demanded complete satisfaction, and Hamilton could not offer humble apologies for remarks he could not recall having made.

Society by this time no longer condoned the duel as a method of settling differences between gentlemen, and civilized people in the United States and Europe considered the practice barbaric. Duels were still fought, to be sure, but by the turn of the nineteenth century one aspect of the unwritten code that governed such engagements was being stressed. For hundreds of years duelists had accepted, in theory, the dictum that honor was satisfied when blood was drawn. Now this rule was considered mandatory, and most duelists, whether fighting with swords or with pistols, tried not to inflict more than superficial flesh wounds on their opponents.

Men who were aware of Aaron Burr's deep and abiding hatred for Alexander Hamilton, however, felt certain that the mere drawing of blood would not satisfy him. From the time they learned of the engagement they were convinced that Burr would shoot to kill, and a number of men, George Clinton among them, spoke of halting a tragedy before it occurred. But no one dared to intervene too openly because of Burr's reputation as a marksman. No man, no matter how high his principles or how great his concern, wanted to be the next target.

On the night of July 10 both of the principals wrote new wills and letters to those closest to them. By an ironic coincidence the duel was scheduled to take place on the deeply wooded heights of Weehawken, New Jersey, on the western hank of the Hudson River, in the precise location where Hamilton's son, Philip, then a youth of twenty, had died in a duel three years earlier.

Billy Van Ness acted as Burr's second, and he was also accompanied in the barge that took him from Richmond Hill to Weehawken by Matthew Davis and another crony from the Tammany Society, Marinus Willett. The duel was scheduled to take place at 7:00 A.M., and the Burr party was the first to arrive, reaching the small clearing in the woods at the crest of the Palisades soon after 6:30. Davis Willett retreated into the woods, and Burr remained with Van Ness. He paced quietly, seemingly at ease, but did not converse.

A few minutes before 7:00 Alexander Hamilton climbed the Palisades, escorted by his second, Judge Nathaniel Pendleton, and by a physician. The seconds shook hands, but the principals confined themselves to brief nods. The rituals of the code of honor were strictly observed. Judge Pendleton asked each of the principals whether their differences could be reconciled and was informed they could not. He carefully explained the rules governing the contest, then inquired if both principals understood what was permitted and what was forbidden, which they did.

Then Burr and Hamilton took their appointed places, and the latter raised his pistol several times to test his aim; he was squinting, and it appeared that the early-morning glare of the sun might be disturbing him. During the few seconds that remained before the duel began, Burr later wrote that his opponent "looked like a convicted felon oppressed with the horrors of conscious guilt." He himself showed no sign of compassion or remorse, either then or at any later date.

When the order to fire was given, both shots sounded simultaneously. Hamilton's aim was wild, and his bullet passed high over his foe's head, clipping a small tree branch, which fell to the ground. Burr, precisely as he expected, hit his mark, the lead ball cutting through Hamilton's ribs on his right side. The impact was so severe that Alexander Hamilton was spun around and faced in the opposite direction as he crumpled. When the smoke cleared away, Burr, his face completely expressionless, watched the physician bending over his fallen enemy.

"This is a mortal wound, Doctor," Hamilton said and lapsed into unconsciousness. Those were the last words he spoke. Although he lingered for twenty-four hours, never regaining consciousness, he died the following day.

Burr returned to Richmond Hill with his friends and displaying a sharp appetite, ate a hearty breakfast. He wrote to Theodosia, telling her briefly that he had won the duel, and for the rest of the day he attended to other correspondence. He was calm, pleasant, and unruffled. At no time did he appear to understand the significance of what he had done.

He soon discovered, however, that the people of the United States could not lightly accept the untimely death of one of the nation's most distinguished citizens and greatest heroes. Americans throughout the country were horrified; Hamilton had been the man who had stood closest to Washington, had done more than any other person to formulate the new

Constitution, and had been the top-ranking officer in the army. The uproar that followed his death was deafening.

Other men, including Mayor De Witt Clinton, of New York City, had killed opponents in duels, and the press had remained silent while the law conveniently looked the other way. But this had been no ordinary duel. Hamilton had been one of the most prominent and highly respected men in the land, whereas Aaron Burr had already earned the contempt of citizens in every state because of his opportunistic switches from one political party to another and the persisting rumors that he had accumulated large sums of money by illegal means. Even more damning, he was universally known as a dead shot with a dueling pistol, so the entire nation realized the killing of Hamilton had been deliberate.

The Federalist newspapers of New York City were the first voices to clamor for the punishment of Hamilton's killer, and within twenty-four hours men of every political persuasion picked up the cry. Burr reacted cynically, attributing the campaign to his many enemies, but he became somewhat confused when the leaders of the Tammany Society joined in the swelling chorus and the rank and file solemnly agreed. Thousands took part in a parade of mourning on the day of Hamilton's funeral.

At the request of a coroner's jury a deputy state's attorney called on Burr and presented him with a charge of murder in the first degree. Van Ness was named as an accomplice but vanished before he could be served, and Davis and Willett were jailed on contempt charges when they refused to testify.

It was impossible to obtain a fair hearing in New York, Burr declared in a hastily written note to his daughter. His political enemies were persecuting him, he said, and had whipped the people into a state of hysteria that defied logic. Other duelists who had won their engagements had not been punished, but he was the butt of lesser men who were jealous of him and feared him.

Having addressed his thoughts to Theodosia and posterity, the Vice-President of the United States slipped away from Richmond Hill in the middle of the night, a fugitive from New York justice. Carrying only two leather boxes filled with clothes, documents, and personal jewelry, he crossed the Hudson to what he believed to be the friendlier shores of New Jersey, then made his way to the Perth Amboy home of an old friend, Navy hero Commodore Thomas Truxton.

He was welcome there, but it quickly became apparent, as news of his arrival spread, that other citizens of the state failed to share Truxton's affection for him. Overnight there were demands for his arrest, and forty-eight hours after his arrival he learned that Bergen County authorities were preparing a warrant charging him with first-degree murder.

Again he fled, this time crossing the border into Pennsylvania. When he reached Philadelphia, he immediately communicated with two of the city's more prominent citizens, Charles Biddle and Alexander Dallas, both of whom had been his staunch supporters in the hotly contested presidential election of 1800-1801. Biddle gave him refuge, and since Alexander Hamilton had never been particularly popular in Philadelphia, he was safe there, at least for the moment.

The newspapers, of course, advertised his presence, and the New York press reported soon thereafter that a band of determined vigilantes was being organized to capture the fugitive, return him to New York, and force him to stand before the bar of justice. Biddle observed that it would be a difficult undertaking, even for the most courageous of men, to attempt his capture.

Burr carried a brace of pistols and his sword at all times, and as an extra precaution, he formed the habit of tucking a slender throwing knife in the top of a boot.

"Those who wish me dead prefer to keep at a very respectful distance," he wrote to Theodosia. "I ride and walk about here as usual."

Taking stock of his situation now that he had a chance to catch his breath, the Vice-President of the United States found little cause for cheer. The New England Federalists reacted to the tragedy with the same horror that filled the rest of the country and instantly abandoned their plans to secede from the Union and form a separate nation. Burr sent them a number of letters which they did not answer, and their silence made it plain they wanted no more to do with him.

The citizens of all the other seaboard states felt the same. Decent men everywhere regarded him as a criminal, and common sense told him that even after the present furor died down, he would find few supporters if he chose to run for elective office. His career in American politics was ended.

His only funds — money he had taken with him when he began his flight — constituted his entire liquid estate, and he read in the New York newspapers that a movement had been initiated to confiscate Richmond Hill, sell the property and its furnishings, and turn over the proceeds to the widowed Mrs. Hamilton and her children. A number of prominent attorneys admitted they doubted the legality of such action, but the people, in their righteous wrath, were capable of doing what they pleased, and Burr realized he had no recourse in the courts.

The law offered him the best hope of salvaging his personal career. Dallas suggested that he open an office in Philadelphia or move to some other state where there was relatively little anti-Burr sentiment. Theodosia wrote to her father, urging a similar plan, and recommended that he practice in Charleston.

The idea of resuming his career as a lawyer did not appeal to Burr. He had breathed the rarefied atmosphere that surrounded men who held high office and found it to his liking. He yearned for power, and nothing else would satisfy him.

Before his departure from Washington City earlier in the year he had held private discussions with the British and Spanish ministers, talking with each about the possibility of working on their behalf for the purpose of expanding their possessions in North America west of the Mississippi. Whether these diplomats seriously entertained his proposals is as difficult to determine today as it was in Aaron Burr's own time. Nevertheless, they listened to him, perhaps because of the novelty of hearing such suggestions made by the second citizen of the United States.

Now, he decided, was the time to renew his proposals, and he sent a carefully worded letter to Anthony Merry, the British minister. This time, however, he changed his tune. Instead of talking in nebulous terms about unexplored territory claimed by several nations, he became far more specific. If the British would provide him with money, ships and munitions, he would form and lead an expedition that would seize the better part of the Louisiana Purchase territories from the United States, and after establishing his headquarters in New Orleans, he would conquer Texas, then a province of Mexico.

In brief, Aaron Burr had finally crossed the line and had become a traitor to his country.

Merry, an honorable man, felt contempt for the schemer, but as a British diplomat it was his duty to explore the idea. Great Britain was worried by the expansion of American territory and the possibility that the new nation might become an important world power. So Merry made a journey to Philadelphia, disguising the purpose of his visit, and in August, 1804, he sat down for a series of secret meetings with Burr, who still held the office of Vice-President of the United States.

As anyone who had heard Burr argue a case in court well knew, there was no more eloquently persuasive speaker in the entire northeastern section of the country. He explained his project in detail, firing Merry with his own enthusiasm, and the minister became convinced that his scheme was feasible. Returning to Washington City, he wrote a long memorandum to his own government, outlining the project and recommending its adoption.

A debate on the merits and demerits of the scheme began in London behind the closed doors of the Crown's ministers. However, events in America were moving too swiftly for men of deliberation to keep pace with them. Burr read in the New York newspapers that his successful opponent in the recent campaign, Governor Morgan Lewis, was planning to submit an official request to Pennsylvania for his extradition, and he realized that his enemies were closing in on him. He was willing to trade blow for blow, shot for shot, with vigilantes who wanted to kidnap him, but as an attorney he knew he was powerless to protect himself from the clutches of the law.

He would have to run away again, this time either to Canada or to the Spanish Floridas. The former would enable him to make his plans with greater ease if the British approved his scheme but would leave him stranded if it was rejected. The campaign against Quebec in 1775 had left him with a strong dislike of Canadian winters, and the Floridas offered a number of possibilities, some of which he had just started to explore. Therefore, he decided to head for the latter region and lost no time in making arrangements to sail on a brig engaged in coastal trade.

No more than an hour or two before his hasty departure he received a letter from Senator Pierce Butler, of Georgia, inviting him to pay a visit to St. Simon, an island off the Georgia coast where the senator owned a plantation. The unexpected gesture during a period when other men shunned him was so flattering that Burr decided to accept, knowing it would be possible for Theodosia and her baby to come from nearby South Carolina for a reunion with him.

He spent fifteen days at sea and was duly deposited at St. Simon. There, to his intense pleasure, he found a royal welcome awaiting him. The dueling code was accepted by virtually all gentlemen in the South, and Burr's host, along with many of his friends, agreed that the Vice-President was the victim of unfair prejudice and persecution. Dinner parties were given in the visitor's honor, he was piled with such thoughtful gifts as a new wardrobe, and his spirits soon revived.

Senator Butler provided him with a house and servants and then filled his larder and wine cellar, so he could return the invitations of the Georgia gentry. Theodosia and her husband, accompanied by their baby, visited him for a week, which enabled him to play the role of the doting grandfather to the hilt.

Burr spent his days at St. Simon hunting, fishing, and boating and after leading a largely sedentary life for years, began to renew the physical vigor and stamina of his youth. He acquired a deep tan, and aside from his increasing baldness, which he did not deign to hide with a wig, he did not look his forty-eight years. Feeling the need for adventure as well as exercise, he made a trip to the Floridas, traveling by canoe and accompanied only by a servant.

What he saw was a Spanish civilization in miniature, set in a vast wilderness, and his ambitious mind gradually turned in a new direction. The scheme that gradually took shape was the most grandiose he had ever dreamed. Even now, more than 150 years later, its full extent is not completely known.

In brief, he reasoned that since the British had not yet responded to his suggested plan, he would also offer his services to Spain. On her supposed behalf he would conquer the Louisiana Territory, formerly a Spanish colony. Then he would take Texas, add it to his growing realm, and push on into Mexico, where he would acquire vast additional territory. Ostensibly, at least in the beginning, he would be acting as Spain's general in the West, but as he gathered strength, land, and riches, he would discard the jurisdiction of feeble, distant Spain and would establish his own empire!

Fantastic as the idea has seemed to generations of historians and students, the discredited, outgoing Vice-President of the United States seriously planned to conquer an empire and establish a personal dynasty, calling himself Aaron I. His son-in-law would succeed him on the throne and would be followed by his grandson, who would be called Aaron II. The very thought of the continuity of the bloodline thrilled him.

Scarcely able to contain his enthusiasm, he hurriedly turned back from the Floridas and traveled to Savannah, where he rented a strong mount for the ride to Charleston. Many historians have said that had his wife still lived, she would have vetoed the entire scheme, calling it impractical and slightly mad. But Burr's daughter had far less influence than his wife and was far more inclined to accept anything he said without question. Theodosia Alston was sparked by her father's excitement and became his first follower. Even the lethargic Alston gave his imagination free rein, and he, too, became a plotter. Since Great Britain, France, and Spain would all benefit from the dismemberment of the United States, Burr intended to solicit funds and other aid from all of them. New Orleans would become his capital, and the European nations that gave him the greatest assistance would be granted special favors in his empire.

Anxious to put his great scheme into operation without delay, he left Charleston and headed northward toward Washington City. Many prominent men in the Carolinas and Virginia were friendly to him, but the climate became cold when he reached Washington City a few weeks before his forty-ninth birthday. Jefferson and Clinton had won a tremendous election victory a few weeks earlier, and the Vice-President-elect, for all practical purposes, had already displaced his predecessor as a citizen of stature.

Few honorable men in the American capital elected to run the risk of being seen in Burr's company, so he found himself virtually an outcast. In addition, the murder indictments obtained by New Jersey and New York were still a factor with which he had to reckon, and both states were certain to demand his extradition. He had also been declared bankrupt by New York. Should he return there, he would find himself in a debtors' prison — if he escaped hanging. Meanwhile, all of his property and possessions, including Richmond Hill and the entire contents of its house and stables, were being auctioned for the benefit of his creditors. He had no funds except a few hundred dollars he had accepted, with a show of reluctance, from his son-in-law before leaving Charleston.

In spite of his crushing difficulties, however, he was still clever enough to outsmart his foes. Until March 4 he still held office as Vice-President of the United States, and since Washington City was federal territory belonging to no state, he enjoyed immunity from arrest and extradition there until the moment George Clinton took the oath of office. So he was free to come and go as he pleased and was in a position to laugh at the New York marshals who had come to escort him to Albany but were forced to return home empty-handed.

Burr's boldness in the face of danger was almost beyond belief. Not only did he dine in the better hotels and taverns of Washington City, but one day in mid-December, 1804, he ascended the Senate rostrum and assumed his vice-presidential role, that of the upper chamber's presiding officer.

The members of the Senate were stunned, and one of the great ironies of American history was a speech made by Senator William Plumer, of New Hampshire, who had been one of the prime Federalist movers of the plan to sever New England and New York from the Union and establish a separate nation. The outraged Plumer declared that this was the first time a murderer had ever presided over the Senate, and he prayed to the Almighty that the United States would never suffer such an embarrassing disgrace again. Many of his colleagues applauded, while the brazen Vice-President smiled down at them from the rostrum.

Aaron Burr was far from friendless during this trying time, however, and the tide began to turn in his favor after James and Dolley Madison, indifferent to criticism, invited him to their home for dinner. Soon thereafter Albert Gallatin dined with him in one of the city's leading taverns, and a few days later the Republican-Democratic majority in the Senate drew up an appeal to the Governor of New Jersey, asking him to quash the murder indictment.

Then President Jefferson himself took a hand in the situation, startling Washington City and the nation by inviting Burr to dine at the President's House. This was the first of several such invitations, all of which were accepted. Both the newly reelected President and the outgoing Vice-President were urbane, sophisticated men, so they were able to chat easily on many subjects. Political matters were not discussed, however, and the name of the late Alexander Hamilton was not mentioned.

Jefferson did more than indicate social sympathy for the man who had risen so high, only to fall so low. The President was making a large number of appointments to federal posts in the Louisiana Territory, and Burr delicately indicated that he would be grateful for inclusion in the patronage. He was invited to submit his suggestions.

To his astonishment, Jefferson accepted all of them. John Barstow Prevost, Burr's stepson, was named as judge of the Superior Court in New Orleans; Joseph Brown, the late Theodosia's former brother-in-law, was nominated for the position of Secretary of Upper Louisiana; and, miracle of miracles, General James Wilkinson, Burr's close friend from their days together in the army and Hamilton's successor as Commander-in-Chief, was nominated by the President for the key post of Governor of the Upper Louisiana District.

Burr and the rawboned Wilkinson renewed their friendship in the early days of 1805; they were birds of a feather, and both recognized their kinship. Wilkinson had been involved in a scandal several years earlier, temporarily losing his commission in the army after engaging in some shady land schemes in which he cheated settlers and Indians alike. Burr knew his friend was ambitious and suspected he had been the primary force responsible for an abortive scheme that would have caused Kentucky to secede from the Union.

Wilkinson's ambitions were, indeed, as great as Burr's, although his talents were fewer, and he suffered from another weakness, too — an addiction to strong drink. One night, while imbibing heavily in the company of his abstemious friend, Wilkinson was led from one step to the next in his discussions with the wily Burr and finally confessed, under an oath of secrecy, that he had long been an agent in the pay of Spain.

Aaron Burr was elated but made no mention of the fact that he had been engaging in a number of private conversations in recent days with an official of the Spanish legation who had visited his quarters late at night. Eventually, without revealing more about his secret plans than was necessary, he enrolled Wilkinson as his own first lieutenant. In return for his services he promised the general a vast domain of his own, which he could rule as he pleased, and the title of first duke of the realm. Like so many others before and after him, James Wilkinson was hypnotized by the smooth, forceful flow of Aaron Burr's electrifying words and imaginative concepts.

Writing to Theodosia and Alston in a newly contrived code, Burr reported the good news. Wilkinson, the future Governor of the entire Upper Louisiana District, was joining them, and his very presence virtually guaranteed the success of the entire scheme.

Burr's love of the theatrical made it impossible for him to disappear quietly from Washington City. He was on the rostrum, as usual, when the Senate convened at noon on March 2, and he quietly announced to the few members present that he had intended to remain until the inauguration of his successor but that a sudden though slight indisposition had forced him to alter his plans. Therefore, with the Senate's indulgence, he wanted to make a few pertinent farewell remarks.

This was an extraordinary occasion, and there was a bustle at the rear of the chamber as pages hurried off to round up absent members. Burr obligingly waited, always preferring as large an audience as it was possible for him to command.

After a delay of five to ten minutes, every member was in his seat, and the press gallery was filled. So many people tried to crowd into the visitors' gallery that another delay ensued while order was restored there.

Then Vice-President Burr delivered his valedictory. At no time in the past four years, he declared, had he knowingly or deliberately offended any senator. It was possible he had erred from time to time, he admitted, but his judgment had always been guided by the rules of parliamentary procedure and, above all, by principle.

For his part, he said, he could complain of no injuries inflicted on him by any member of the Senate, and, he added, he was thankful to God that he had no memory for injuries.

He and the members of the Senate were parting now, he declared, probably forever. He was leaving with the deepest personal affection for every senator and offered his prayers and most earnest wishes for their separate and joint well-being.

Finally, his voice rising, he concluded his brief address:

> This house is a sanctuary; a citadel of law, of order, and of liberty; it is here — it is here in this exalted refuge — here, if anywhere, will be resistance made to the storms of political frenzy and the silent arts of corruption. And if the Constitution be destined ever to perish by the sacrilegious hands of the demagogue or the usurper, which God avert, its expiring agonies will be witnesses on this floor.
>
> I shall, until I die, feel reverence for this house and the noble principles of which it is the primary guardian. In taking my leave of it and of you, I feel like the young man who leaves the dwelling of his parents to make his way in the

world. This house is my mother, and has nurtured me; this house is my father, and has given me strength.

May the Almighty bless you and keep you in all that you do together here and separately in your own homes. I ask only that you not forget me, for I, of a certainty, shall always remember, with respect and affection, the years I spent here.

There was a moment of silence, then Burr bowed, turned, and abruptly walked up the center aisle and left the chamber.

The members of the United States Senate rose as one and rendered him a standing ovation.

As he left the Capitol, cheers were still resounding for a patriot who had been rehabilitated in the eyes of his peers. As soon as he reached the street, however, he knew that his status had changed. He was a refugee who enjoyed immunity from arrest, at least in Washington City, for slightly less than forty-eight hours. He could see no bailiffs from either New York or New Jersey lying in wait for him, but he was taking no unnecessary chances, and his complicated plans were already made.

He left the Capitol on horseback, changed to another horse at the stable behind a small inn, and subsequently was believed to have transferred again, this time to a coach with heavy, closed curtains. Then he disappeared from sight.

Two days later he reappeared at the home of Dallas in Philadelphia. He had made his arrangements with great care, and a few hours later he was deep in conference with the British minister, Anthony Merry, who had also left Washington City and had come to Philadelphia for the express purpose of holding these talks. The two men did not meet in the home of Dallas, who knew nothing of Aaron's plans and would have been compromised if they were exposed. Besides, being a patriotic citizen, Dallas undoubtedly would have carried the sensational tale to the government.

No one has ever learned where the conferences took place, but Merry's confidential reports to his superiors in London indicate their substance. Burr was making specific plans now and knew precisely what he wanted. In order to conquer the West, including both American and Spanish territory, and push on to establish a Mexican empire which included the province of Texas, he needed two heavily armed frigates, four or five smaller war vessels, and the loan of £100,000, which he promised to repay with interest when he established his own nation and became its monarch.

His unbridled imagination had already created that realm in his mind, and he told Merry something of the country he expected to found. He would be an emperor or a king, to be sure, but would not become a despot; on the contrary, he envisioned his nation as a benevolent autocracy. He would be aided by a parliament founded on what he called a "true democratic" basis. His chief advisers would sit in a house of peers, but the nobles would not hold their seats because of their wealth and power. Their achievements would win them these places, and he hoped that philosophers and teachers, authors and artists, would join distinguished statesmen, diplomats, and soldiers there. In fact, he planned to offer inducements to the prominent men of many lands in order to persuade them to migrate to his new kingdom.

There would be a lower house in his parliament, too, made up of representatives elected by the ordinary citizens. He did not dwell on the functions of this chamber, but Merry gathered it would have no powers other than those of offering advice to the monarch and his cabinet. As nearly as Merry could glean, the dreamer intended to use the lower chamber as something of a sounding board.

Burr's plans for the actual establishment of his empire were even more specific. He had convinced himself that the people of the American West felt no loyalty to the United States and would be eager to join him. He would prepare the ground himself, and at the appropriate time the people of New Orleans, who had known Spanish and French rule prior to the Louisiana Purchase, would declare themselves independent of the United States. Their city would become the capital of the new realm.

The Louisiana back country, always ruled by New Orleans, would be certain to follow the lead of the city. At the same time Kentucky and Tennessee would secede from the Union and join the new nation. He hoped that Ohio would do the same but admitted to the British minister that he was relatively unfamiliar with the sentiments of men in the Ohio country and therefore could not be certain of their reaction.

These peaceful declarations would be a signal to General Wilkinson, who would march with a small military force into Texas, which he would annex. Then, depending upon conditions in the field, he would push on deeper into Mexico, annexing additional territory "wherever he finds that the people will welcome" the founding of this new utopia.

Everything depended on the aid that Great Britain was willing to give him, as well as his own ability to neutralize the Spanish forces in North America. He reasoned that Britain, at war with France and French-dominated Spain and also on less than amiable terms with the United States, would be happy to cooperate. As for Spain, both he and General Wilkinson were emphasizing to officials of the Spanish legation in Washington City that they were working on Madrid's behalf. The Spanish diplomats appeared to have been taken in by the ruse; indeed, they were promising their help and, perhaps, their money in the venture.

Burr bolstered his arguments with Merry by promising that Great Britain would have special rights as a trading partner and would be able to obtain the products and natural resources of his realm at a price lower than any other nation would be charged. This, in turn, would enable Canada to grow stronger at the expense of the United States, too, and he placed special emphasis on the partnership between his nation and Canada.

Minister Merry suffered no false illusions regarding the character of the man with whom he was dealing. He regarded Aaron Burr as "the king of rascals," according to a letter he sent to the Foreign Office in London. The man was totally lacking in conscience and was completely untrustworthy because his ambitions were boundless, and he would do anything he found desirable or necessary to achieve them.

All the same, Merry recognized Burr's enormous talents. He was a dreamer, to be sure, but he was a man capable of making those dreams come true, and the results would be of great benefit to Britain — at small cost. He was sufficiently impressed by the elaborate plot to recommend that Britain accept the bargain and act accordingly. He also made the mistake of telling Burr what he was recommending.

Eagerness to put his design into operation at the earliest possible moment caused Aaron Burr to confuse the will with the deed. Although the British government had taken no action whatever on his grandiose proposal, which was still under consideration, he regarded Anthony Merry's approval as being tantamount to the official sanction of His Majesty's cabinet.

Not only was he unwilling to wait, but the knowledge that New York might request his extradition at any moment made him all the more determined to act with dispatch. By early April news of his presence in Philadelphia had become common knowledge, even though he rarely left Dallas's home, and he was afraid that if he lingered much longer, he would be cast in prison.

Accordingly, in the latter part of April, 1805, he set out on the greatest venture of his life — one that would, if successful, place a crown on his head.

Chapter 12

Ordinary men expected to endure hardships when they traveled through the wilderness of North America, but the future emperor of the West was no ordinary man, at least by his own standards. Still living on borrowed money, Aaron Burr wrote ahead to Pittsburgh, and for less than $150 a special riverboat was built to his specifications. Made of seasoned oak, it was sixty feet long and fourteen feet wide. Among other features it contained a sitting room, a dining room, a kitchen complete with a brick fireplace, two full bedrooms, and "space sufficient to house her captain and crew."

He rode westward across the mountains to Pittsburgh, and his story varied from stop to stop, depending on the character and interests of his listeners. He told some that he hoped to start life anew in the West: He intended to carve a new home for himself in the wilderness and assist in the growth of the territory. If all went well, perhaps he would be fortunate someday and be sent by the citizens of a new state to the Senate or the House of Representatives. When he stayed overnight with merchants or traders, the story was altered. These worthy citizens were informed that he was penniless, which was true, and that he hoped to earn a new fortune for himself in a portion of the country remote from the enemies who had ruined him.

Nowhere did he breathe a word of his conspiracy. People in this part of the United States were good citizens, and many — particularly the Virginians who had settled in the western portion of Pennsylvania — were fiercely loyal to President Jefferson.

At Pittsburgh he was joined by Congressman Matthew Lyon, of Tennessee, one of his staunchest supporters in the federal government. They traveled together for a short time, but Lyon was bewildered and somewhat irritated by Burr's leisurely pace. Finally it occurred to Lyon that there might be more to this journey than was visible on the surface, and Burr was undoubtedly relieved when the congressman decided to move ahead on his own.

The people of the West were anxious to see the former Vice-President, the man who had killed Alexander Hamilton and ruined his own good name. Crowds awaited him in such towns as Wheeling and Marietta, and Burr made it his custom to come ashore from his houseboat, make an informal speech, and mingle with the throngs. He was so affable that the Westerners felt certain many lies had been told about him: Here was no aristocrat, but a man in homespun clothes who happily rubbed shoulders with them, exchanged jokes, and put on no airs. Aaron Burr was a man after their own hearts, and in town after town he was urged to become a settler.

Had Aaron Burr accepted one of these invitations, he might well have become a spokesman for the West, which was desperately seeking leaders of national stature who could explain and fight for the western point of view in the nation's councils. Many were aware of this vacuum, although Burr was not among them, having been blinded by his own overweening ambition. Within a few years the vacancies would be filled by two of the most prominent men in American history — Andrew Jackson, of Tennessee, and Henry Clay, of Kentucky.

The houseboat glided down the Ohio River, and reaching a place called Backus Island, located in the center of the broad stream, Aaron Burr saw a huge house, which resembled a New England mansion, perched high on a bluff. The place was the home of an eccentric, wealthy genius, Harman Blennerhassett, who had inherited a fortune, had no need to earn a living, and spent all of his time on his hobbies, which included chemistry, astronomy, and music. This university-trained Irish immigrant, who lived with his wife and strapping sons, was endowed with a vivid imagination and had ample funds to indulge in caprice.

Burr went ashore, intending to remain for a few hours, and instead stayed for several days. By the time he left, Blennerhassett and his sons had become active participants in the conspiracy.

When the wayfarer reached Cincinnati, he became the house guest of Senator John Smith, of Ohio, who was entertaining another guest — former Senator Jonathan Dayton, of New Jersey. Dayton was a sensitive, forceful man, and having lost a fortune which he was trying to recoup, he was susceptible to new ideas.

Dayton and Burr had sat at adjoining desks in the Senate during the Washington administration, had become well acquainted, and still felt great respect for each other. As it developed, Burr placed greater trust in the vigorous, handsome Dayton than in anyone else who knew about his plot. Unburdening himself without reservation, the former Vice-President revealed the complete details of the grand design to the former senator. They soon struck a bargain: Dayton, in return for his active cooperation, would become prime minister of the yet to be established empire.

Dayton stayed behind to obtain additional recruits in political, financial, and business circles, while Burr continued his westward journey. Reaching Louisville, where he received a particularly warm reception, he left his boat in the care of friends, then went on to Tennessee on horseback.

In both Kentucky and Tennessee he encountered many men who spoke openly of leaving the Union and forming a new nation. In fact, a portion of Tennessee, which had called itself the state of Franklin for a number of years, had been on the verge of secession before the territory had been reorganized pending the admission of the entire area to statehood under a different name.

The frontiersmen of these western states would make ideal recruits, and Burr was quick to recognize their potential worth to him. They were fiercely independent, courageous to a fault, and were bound to the federal government of the United States by few ties. Almost all were self-reliant and if subjected to discipline, would make superb soldiers, since they were all familiar with firearms.

Wherever Burr went on his journey, he halted for visits and speech-making, and it is unfortunate that no texts of these addresses have survived. According to the accounts of men who heard him, he was simultaneously forceful and subtle. Not once did he openly advocate that Kentucky and Tennessee secede from the Union, but his audiences instantly grasped the meaning of his hints and roared their approval.

"In Frankfort and Lexington," he wrote Theodosia, "I was received with the adulation that, in a monarchy, is reserved for a king admired, respected and loved by all."

Tennessee gave him an even more royal welcome. In 1791 he had been one of the few members of the Senate to favor the admission of Franklin to the Union as a state, and since that time he had been consistent in his advocacy of the region's interests. In addition, the killing of Alexander Hamilton was not regarded as a stigma in this part of the country, where duels were fought often. Furthermore, Hamilton had been regarded as the champion of the East, so the man who had dispatched him with a neatly placed bullet was considered a hero.

Hundreds of parading militiamen and other citizens escorted the visitor in triumph to their showplace — the new red-brick Nashville Inn, supposedly the best hostelry in the West. In Washington City Burr had been friendly with Senator Andrew Jackson, who was now the commander of the Tennessee militia, and after a well-attended banquet was given in Burr's honor, the impetuous Jackson took him off in triumph to the Hermitage, his own home outside the city.

There one of Jackson's close friends and subordinates, Colonel John Coffee, the militia's cavalry commander, chatted for the better part of the night. The general and the colonel drank copious quantities of whiskey, but their guest, ever careful, confined himself to a single glass.

Burr later wrote that as the night wore on, he was tempted to reveal at least the broad outlines of his plan to the two Tennesseans. But he obeyed his instinct, which cautioned him to say nothing. Had he talked about his scheme, even in the vaguest terms, that would have been the end of his conspiracy. Andrew Jackson — as he would amply demonstrate before, during, and following his two terms as President of the United States — loved his country with unmatched ferocity. The giant Coffee was an American patriot, too, and would have joined the rawboned, ugly Jackson in apprehending the traitor had either suspected his plans.

But Aaron Burr charmed them, as he charmed so many others, and the following day Jackson provided him with a barge and a military escort for his journey. The militiamen not only protected the distinguished visitor but sailed the barge, cooked his meals, and made him comfortable.

After a journey of two hundred miles on the winding Cumberland River, Burr reached a military post, Fort Massac, near what later became Cairo, Illinois, where another distinguished American awaited him. He went at once into private conference with Brigadier General James Wilkinson, Commander-in-Chief of the Army and Federal Governor of the Upper Louisiana Territory.

Here the conspirators perfected and polished their plans. The British loan had not yet materialized, and money was badly needed, but Burr was not deterred by the facts of the situation. He recounted British Minister Merry's enthusiasm, and as far as he was concerned, British warships were already sailing across the Atlantic to assist him, and British gold would soon be jingling in his purse.

Wilkinson gave Burr two important letters of introduction to use in New Orleans. One was addressed to the Marquis de Casa Yrujo, the Spanish high commissioner in New Orleans, and read: "Serve this gentleman as you would serve me, and the great interest of your country will be served."

The other communication was addressed to Daniel Clark, a wealthy New Orleans merchant who owned a fleet of commercial ships and vast warehouses in the city. It was equally succinct: "This will be delivered to you by Colonel Burr. To him I refer you for many things improper to letter."

The scheme was taking shape rapidly. Clark was one of the largest landowners in Mexico and lived in constant fear that the government there would seize his property. It would not be difficult to win his cooperation and, hopefully, a cash contribution to the Burr-Wilkinson cause. The marquis should prove a willing ally, too, and Burr hoped to gain as much as possible from him.

General Wilkinson planned to return to his own headquarters in St. Louis. There, he believed, he was making progress in his attempt to persuade a number of his key junior officers that it would be worth their while to join him on an expedition into Texas.

Burr sailed down the Mississippi River on a magnificent barge that Wilkinson had ordered built for him as a surprise gift. A sergeant in the United States Army was in command, and ten soldiers of the regular force manned the vessel, which was more like a houseboat than a barge. While on board he slept, ate his meals, and wrote letters in a suite of three large comfortable rooms, which were placed at his disposal.

Arriving at Natchez on June 17, he spoke with greater candor to the crowds that gathered to honor him. Although he still exercised a measure of care, a number of listeners grasped his ultimate intentions. It has been said that the failure of the conspiracy was caused by Aaron Burr's seeming inability to remain silent long enough. Certainly his address to the people of Natchez was a blunder. Rumors about his plans began to circulate widely, and eventually the whispers reached the eastern seaboard.

New Orleans outdid even Natchez in the warmth of its welcome, and large numbers of all three major ethnic groups in the city were on hand to greet Aaron Burr. General Wilkinson's agents had done their work well, and the ground was thoroughly prepared. The marquis had passed the word that the former Vice-President was the great friend of the Spanish-speaking community. Those who spoke French had been informed he was their champion and had fought for their interests in Washington City. W. C. Claiborne, the United States Governor of the Orleans Territory, was almost overcome by the honor of entertaining such a noted guest and made a welcoming speech that lasted forty-five minutes.

Daniel Clark was delighted with the scheme when Burr filled him in on the details and not only pledged his own cooperation but brought a number of other merchants into the conspiracy, all of them having business interests in Mexico. Another welcome and important addition to the growing list was an organization known as the Mexican Society, a group of American businessmen, war veterans, and adventurers whose common aim — openly expressed — was the annexation of that entire country.

Events moved swiftly, and Aaron was elated because all the pieces of his design were falling into their appropriate places. The Mexican Society sent several secret agents — men familiar with Mexico — across the border to enlist allies and prepare for the coming of what was already being termed a "liberty army." Daniel Clark demonstrated his wholehearted support of the project by giving Burr three large detailed maps, which were far superior to any already in the possession of the future emperor or General Wilkinson. Clark also pledged financial support, giving Burr $25,000 in cash and promising a similar sum at a later date. Several of his friends also donated a joint gift of $25,000 and declared they would donate an extra $50,000 when more money was needed.

At no time in his turbulent life was Aaron Burr's warped genius more evident. He ignored no segment of New Orleans society, and in the seventeen days he spent in the city he won the confidence of some of the community's most influential men. Southern Louisiana was predominantly Roman Catholic, and the man who had been a freethinker since his undergraduate days expressed his admiration for Catholicism with such sincerity that he won the friendship of the bishop.

He also charmed the Jesuits, and these usually wise men enlisted in his cause with such enthusiasm that they sent several emissaries into Mexico to prepare the Spanish-speaking population for the coming of their "friends," the regiments of the liberty army.

The crowds that saw Burr off at the riverfront when he departed on his barge on July 10 were even larger than the throngs that had greeted him on his arrival. He retraced the steps of his journey in the opposite direction, certain in his own mind that within a year his empire would be established. One man who failed to share his optimism was the Marquis de Casa Yrujo, a shrewd diplomat who knew the New World and its people. He had agreed with everything Burr had said to him, but his reports to his own superiors in Madrid told a far different story.

He called the expedition into Mexico ridiculous and chimerical. Under no circumstances could it succeed, he wrote, and he very much doubted that it would ever be undertaken. He also revealed the complicated deviousness of the game General Wilkinson was playing. According to his reports, Wilkinson was revealing to him all that Aaron Burr was planning; apparently the general believed from the outset that the dream was beyond realization, so he was taking care to protect his own flanks.

Burr, of course, was not aware of this development and could scarcely contain his excitement when he reached Washington City in mid-November. He paid an immediate visit to the British legation, going there late one evening. After telling Minister Merry about the great success he had enjoyed to date, he confidently inquired when the British warships and cash loan would be forthcoming. Merry did not know and added that he had no idea whether his superiors in London had approved of the entire plan or had rejected it. He had made a number of inquiries, but his superiors had not chosen to reply.

For the moment, at least, Aaron Burr was stunned. He had been counting on the British loan, even though the generosity of Daniel Clark and the other New Orleans merchants had alleviated his immediate financial needs. The loss of the British warships was a more severe blow, and he frantically began to search for other ways to put together his personal navy. What really disturbed him was the realization that Great Britain, the most powerful nation on earth, lacked faith in his dream.

Chapter 13

Jonathan Dayton, who had reached Washington City a few weeks before Aaron Burr's arrival, shared his coconspirator's dismay, and the would-be emperor sat down with his future prime minister for a review of the entire situation. It was quite apparent that perfidious Albion would not help them, so they wrote off British gold, ships, and friendship. Other sources of funds and frigates were available, and the Marquis de Casa Yrujo, having been transferred from New Orleans to Washington City, became their prime target.

They laid a trap for him, baiting it with a mixture of facts and lies. They had been disappointed by Great Britain, Dayton informed the Spanish minister, and consequently were changing their plans. Since it would be impossible for them to take an expedition into Mexico, they would turn in the opposite direction. Colonel Burr and his associates would lead the American West in an uprising, capture Washington City, and then imprison President Jefferson, along with all other members of the federal government, whose places they would appropriate. The Spanish colonies of North America would no longer be in danger, and Colonel Burr, who would make himself President of the United States for life, would become Spain's sworn ally.

The very idea of such a scheme was absurd, and no one knew it better than Burr and Dayton, who had no real intention of trying to carry out such a plan. Their real goals remained unaltered. They still intended to carve their own empire out of the Louisiana Purchase lands, Texas, and parts of Mexico. The mad notion they presented to the Spanish minister was meant to dupe him into giving them support, and in this maneuver they succeeded brilliantly.

It is difficult to understand, in the latter part of the twentieth century, how any experienced diplomat could have been taken in by such gibberish, but the Marquis de Casa Yrujo swallowed the bait without hesitation. His gullibility can be explained on several grounds. The age was one of intrigue, in which boundaries were constantly being changed, as were the sovereignty over large New World territories. Not only had the United States itself come into existence within the last thirty years, but the Louisiana Territory had belonged to three countries — Spain, France, and the United States — in the minister's own adult lifetime. He was familiar with the yearnings for total independence that manifested themselves in the American West and had witnessed the abortive state of Franklin's attempt to secede from the Union. He also knew that the Federalists of New England had planned to break away from the United States, changing their minds abruptly after Alexander Hamilton's death.

Therefore he could accept the Burr-Dayton blueprint at face value. The marquis liked to think of himself as a shrewd judge of human character, and he had correctly recognized the ruthless qualities that would have enabled Aaron Burr to carry out such a plot, had that been his real intention. It may have been this awareness that convinced him the plan well might succeed.

Whatever his reasons may have been, the Spanish minister became enthusiastic. He believed the project would be simple to bring off, largely because the United States government lived in blissful ignorance of the threat to its security. He sent a firm recommendation to Madrid, requesting that the huge sum of $500,000 be given to Colonel Burr for the purchase of arms and ships and for recruiting an army. In fact, he placed so much trust in the conspirators that Dayton was allowed to read the marquis's report to his own government before it was dispatched.

Atlantic crossings were necessarily slow, and a ship sailing to a Spanish port from the United States could not be expected to reach its destination in less than a month. Consequently many weeks would go by before the minister could expect to receive a reply from Madrid. This time lag worried Yrujo. In fact, he was so fearful that Burr and Dayton might lose heart prematurely that in a gesture of encouragement and faith, he advanced them the sum of five thousand dollars out of his own pocket.

Burr's correspondence with his fellow conspirators during this period, all of it written in various complicated codes, indicates no lessening of his own optimism. The loss of Great Britain as a sponsor did not upset him, because he had found another patron in Spain, and consequently only a few minor changes in tactics were required. The lure of empire still beckoned; he would make New Orleans his capital, and his personal monarchy would become the most powerful and enlightened in the New World.

He made only one error in his calculations at this time, but it was a major one. Foolishly, almost blindly, he clung to the belief that his entire plot remained a closely guarded secret known only to a small handful of reliable men. It was true, to be sure, that the details of his scheme had not leaked out, but he failed to take into consideration the common sense of the American people.

His valedictory to the Senate had lulled many men, and for a short time he had been almost universally regarded as a patriot whose labors on behalf of his country had been misunderstood and misinterpreted. His trip into the West had been regarded as the first, necessary move in an attempt to rehabilitate himself, and even men who had disliked him had wished him well. Now, however, he had returned to Washington City and was lingering there for no discernible reason — an affable, charming, and closemouthed man who discussed his future only in vague terms and refused to be pinned down when asked about his plans.

Many prominent New Englanders and New Yorkers were aware of his previous attempt to lead a secession movement. Many others, among them Albert Gallatin, had known him to break promises. Moreover, the entire country had seen him leaping nimbly from one political party to another, taking up temporary residence under the roof that afforded him the best shelter at any given moment. Finally, President Jefferson had good reason to look at his former Vice-President with a jaundiced eye.

Dayton and Wilkinson may have been the only men familiar with the entire plan churning in Burr's mind, but there were many others, particularly in the states and territories of the West, who knew portions of the overall design. The New Orleans merchants who had already advanced money for his cause could not keep silent; planters at Natchez and other towns who had heard Aaron speak had no reason to refrain from revealing what they had learned.

Bits of the puzzle made their way to the major cities of the United States, located on the eastern seaboard. Rumors abounded. In or out of the government Aaron Burr was one of the most forceful and colorful men in the United States, so it was inevitable that people should wonder and talk about him. Speculation crept into print, and newspapers in a score of communities began to ask questions, some of them striking dangerously close to the mark.

Why had Colonel Burr gone West, only to return East? What was he doing in Washington City? Why had he become so friendly with various officials of the Spanish legation? Could it be true, as people were saying in New Orleans, that he hoped to wage a private war against Mexico? And suppose he conquered the Mexicans — what would he do with the territory he acquired?

Burr read many of these newspaper accounts and should have been alarmed by them. Had he been alert to danger, he would have stepped up his timetable and acted before the suspicions of the American government and public became too widespread. But his self-confidence was so great that he had become arrogant, and his letters to his daughter in the winter of 1805-1806 reveal no reaction except tolerant amusement. People were speculating about him, and many of the guesses were fairly accurate, but mere gossip could not hurt him.

He was wrong. Perhaps his greatest weakness was his total inability to judge the temperament of the American people. In his opinion the public could be fooled, swayed, and led at will, and he clung to that view, even though his repeated failure to win major elections should have caused him to reevaluate his judgments. What he did not and apparently could not grasp was that the people were watching him, waiting to pounce when he erred.

His careless indifference to the talk about him may have grown out of his increasing contempt for American authority. The indictments against him in New York and New Jersey had not been quashed, but neither state made any attempt to extradite him, and he interpreted their failure to act against him as a fatal sign of weakness. What he failed to realize was that new social, political, and economic problems were occupying the time and attention of the people, and the governments of New York and New Jersey did not wish to be embarrassed by a trial that would awaken old enmities and passions. An impotent Aaron Burr — private citizen, a man who held no office and gave no indication of wanting to hold office — was harmless, and both states were willing to forget the past, provided Burr behaved himself.

He knew only that he was safe, that no one wanted to arrest him, and that he was free to go where he pleased. Yrujo's loan enabled him to live in style, and he spent the winter daydreaming and trying to make those dreams come true. He needed competent lieutenants, especially experienced soldiers and sailors, and he realized that his navy would be his greatest weakness now that Great Britain refused to support him.

So it was natural for him to approach his friend, Commodore Thomas Truxton, who had given him refuge in New Jersey after he had fled from New York. Truxton had been pushed into what he considered premature retirement by President Jefferson and consequently loathed the nation's Chief Executive, so Aaron considered him the ideal candidate for the post of naval commander.

They met in Washington City at Burr's request, and he asked his friend if he would be willing to resign from the United States Navy, take command of a private expedition, and become the permanent head of the naval forces of a new about-to-be-created nation. Truxton's reply was blunt: Regardless of his personal opinion of Thomas Jefferson, he owed allegiance only to the United States and would obey any order given him by his nation's President. He would fight to defend the United States in a war with Great Britain, France,

Spain, or any other nation, including a newly established country.

Burr retreated with as much grace as he could muster. He had badly misinterpreted the character of Commodore Truxton and for the first time was afraid he had revealed too much about his grandiose plans. But Truxton regarded him as a harmless, idle dreamer and did not pass along any details of the conversation to anyone else.

The next recruit to be solicited for support was William Eaton, a self-styled general and one of the most curious figures in American history. Eaton, who had held a minor diplomatic post in North Africa, had chosen to ignore the fact that he was in the employ of the State Department rather than the War Department. Acting on his own initiative, he had led an expedition across the sands of the North African desert and had forced the capitulation of the pirate government of Tripoli, which had been holding the officers and seamen of the captured U.S. *Philadelphia* as prisoners. The American people regarded Eaton as a hero, although the Jefferson administration was embarrassed by his antics. State governments had heaped honors on him and had made him gifts of valuable tracts of land, but the federal government had ignored him, and he was now in Washington City trying to obtain repayment of the funds he had spent out of his own pocket for his expedition.

Eaton was a talented man, but his success in North Africa had caused him to entertain an inflated opinion of his own prowess. Although he listened to Burr's proposition, he had no intention of acknowledging General Wilkinson as his superior officer. He was not lacking in patriotism, although he was guilty of muddled thinking, so he tried to solve the problem in his own way. Colonel Burr's scheme would be aborted, he believed, if the colonel was sent out of the country, and the best way to persuade him to leave would be the brilliant stratagem of offering him a diplomatic plum. If he were made United States Minister to Great Britain or Spain, for example, he might be induced to forget his wild plan.

For his own devious reasons Burr encouraged Eaton. If he should be appointed the top United States representative in London or Madrid, he would be in a position to pursue his own designs without hindrance from anyone, and he felt certain he could personally persuade either Britain or Spain to become his active partners in the establishment of his empire.

Congratulating himself on his own wisdom, Eaton went to the President with his suggestion, but Jefferson calmly declined to appoint Aaron Burr to any diplomatic post. Eaton failed to take advantage of his opportunity to tell the President all he knew of the plot and just backed away from his request. He felt, as Truxton had, that Aaron Burr was harmless and that his scheme would collapse.

It was difficult for an impatient man to wait week after endless week for word from Madrid, but Burr had no alternative. Actually, the Spanish government sent no reply to the Marquis de Casa Yrujo until the early summer of 1806. That reply was succinct: Under no circumstances would one copper be provided for Colonel Burr's mad venture.

Many schemers would have given up after this latest rebuff, but Burr once again demonstrated that he was no ordinary mortal. He had already made emergency plans and promptly put them into operation. First he borrowed substantial sums from his son-in-law, from one Daniel Smith, from Blennerhassett, and even from Dayton. Then he formed a land company in the West, and although his claim to various properties in the Louisiana Territory was flimsy, he began to sell homesteads to men who wanted to settle there. He needed neither Britain nor Spain, would attend to all of the financing himself, and would be beholden to no one. Then, when his empire came into existence, he would force London and Madrid to pay dearly for their snubs.

Dayton was committed to the enterprise with all his heart, but General Wilkinson, decoding long letters in distant St. Louis, began to entertain strong doubts. The delays were infuriating, his own ambitions were not being satisfied, and he began to wonder whether Burr would ever put his scheme into operation. He began to think that it was far better to serve himself — to await the right opportunity and then lead an expedition into Texas under his own banner.

Aware of Wilkinson's dwindling enthusiasm, Burr enlisted Dayton's aid in trying to rekindle the general's interest. These efforts failed, and knowing he needed the general, he threatened to "dismiss" him. It was a hollow gesture, however, and had no effect other than to render Wilkinson even more reluctant to remain a member of the conspiracy.

Then, unexpectedly, in midsummer of 1806, events beyond Aaron Burr's control made it possible for him to spring into action. A growing dispute with Spain compelled the peace-loving Thomas Jefferson to send the army into the field so that in the event of a Spanish invasion, the enemy could be thrust back across the border. This was the perfect excuse to march into Texas — and beyond.

Burr immediately sent a long, flattering letter to Wilkinson, urging him to put their plan into operation while he himself followed with additional recruits. Letters went to several cronies in New York and elsewhere, each of whom promised to bring in his share of young men eager for adventure and glory. In all, 150 volunteers signed for the march, but Burr took care not to let them know his ultimate aims. They were told only that they would settle on a vast tract of land owned by Colonel Burr in the Louisiana Territory, and "if conditions should permit," they would take part in a foreign expedition that would win them wealth and fame.

Blennerhassett's island was designated as the rendezvous, and Burr left Washington City for his appointment with destiny, traveling alone. Dayton rode ahead, following another route, the two principal conspirators having decided that for safety's sake they would not go together on the first leg of their journey through the relatively heavily populated farm country of Pennsylvania.

Two other travelers who hurried from South Carolina to Pittsburgh were Theodosia and Aaron Burr Alston, the young woman responding to an urgent summons from her father. Burr wanted his family with him on what he saw as the climactic chapter of his adventure. His son-in-law stayed behind in Charleston because he was too ill to travel. He was afflicted with a severe case of the ague, later called influenza. Actually Alston was fortunate to be confined to his bed. Had he accompanied his wife and child, whom he intended to join at a later date, he would have lost his good name, too, by the time the final act in the tragedy was played.

Burr now shook off the lethargy that had gripped him during his final months in Washington City. He was on the road, in action at last, and once again was the magnetic leader of men who had inspired his troops at Quebec and in the Battle of Monmouth. Fiery and persuasive in all encounters along the way, he succeeded in picking up a dozen more recruits, and the ranks were augmented by an additional twenty men after he reached Pittsburgh.

Once again, however, Aaron Burr misjudged the character of the American people. Admittedly those who joined him were semiliterate farmers and sons of farmers, but they were not stupid. Many of them read between the lines of his recruiting speeches, speculated about the nature of his real intentions, and passed along their suspicions to county supervisors, circuit court judges, and other officials they knew and trusted. While Burr lingered for a few days in Pittsburgh, celebrating his reunion with his beloved daughter and grandson, at least nine Pennsylvanians who held positions of authority and trust in state or local governments sent urgent letters to friends in Washington City, warning that Aaron Burr was up to no good and should be watched.

Chapter 14

By the middle of September, 1806, Blennerhassett's island had become an armed camp. Two hundred men, their ranks growing daily, drilled with muskets and fired the three cannons that Jonathan Dayton had acquired in some mysterious fashion. Silos were built for the corn and wheat, jerked beef, and dried fish that were delivered each day by boat. Armed guards stood sentry duty at the arsenal, formerly a barn, where lead and bags of gunpowder were stored.

Every day, promptly at noon, the garrison paraded under the critical eye of the future emperor, whose daughter and grandson usually stood beside him and took the salute with him. Aaron Burr was riding high, certain in his own mind that he was on the verge of fulfilling his destiny. He wrote more openly to Wilkinson, who was already on the march in accordance with President Jefferson's instructions, and to Dayton, who had gone ahead to Louisville and Nashville. What need was there to write in code when victory was assured?

Burr left Blennerhassett's island ahead of his little army, and as he traveled on the familiar route through Kentucky and Tennessee, his tactics became bolder and more careless. A member of his entourage, unidentified down to the present day, wrote a set of forged orders which bore the signature of Jefferson's Secretary of War, General Henry Dearborn. These documents purported to name Aaron Burr a major general in the United States Army and authorized him to raise a corps of troops for the purpose of making secret preparations for war against Mexico.

The documents looked authentic, no one who saw them knew Secretary Dearborn's signature, and so many recruits flocked to Burr's banner that he was forced to send word ahead to General Andrew Jackson in Nashville, requesting the building of a large fleet of flatboats to transport his corps. Jackson, who had no reason to suspect a conspiracy, displayed his usual gusto, and not only had the flatboats built in record time, but accumulated additional stores of munitions and food for the man he regarded as a patriotic colleague.

The success of this deception was so great that Burr stepped up the pace of his correspondence with the inflammable Jackson, and when he wrote that Spanish troops had already crossed the Mississippi River border in several places, the eager Jackson called up his Tennessee militia to meet the challenge.

On the last day of September Aaron Burr arrived in Nashville. That night a banquet was given in his honor. He offered a toast to the total defeat of the Spaniards, and his audience cheered so loudly that it became virtually impossible to restore order for the rest of the evening.

By this time he had concocted his final plans, which were as simple as they were audacious. General Wilkinson would lead the march into Texas with his vanguard of United States Army regulars. Burr, who would have established his own headquarters in New Orleans by that time, would follow with his own corps, which he estimated would number approximately one thousand men. He needed no more, he reasoned, because the leadership of the corps would be superb: He would attend to that chore himself, and he was convinced that battles, campaigns, and wars were won by the brilliance of commanding generals, not by sheer numbers.

Sooner or later, he realized, the federal government in Washington City would learn of his deception, but he was

160

gambling that it would then be too late to stop him. If his luck held, he would march into Mexico by the end of the year and destroy the inferior Mexican forces located there before Washington City could interfere. That victory would make him a hero to his followers, and he was confident the American people would approve, too.

At that critical moment he would announce the establishment of his empire. He had no doubt that some of his troops were patriotic American citizens who would balk, but he would use his best oratory in an attempt to persuade them to join him. Those who refused would be free to cross the border and return to the United States. Meanwhile, the American public would be so enthralled by his victory that it would be impossible for Jefferson or any other President to persuade the Congress to declare war against him and send an expedition to chastise him.

He was so proud of himself that he could not resist boasting in the letters he sent to Theodosia, who had stayed behind at Blennerhassett's island. He had taken care to cover every angle and had found snug plugs to fill every loophole. His triumph would be all the more miraculous and all the sweeter because he would have achieved it alone, fighting against odds that lesser men would have regarded as insurmountable.

On October 1, 1806, he wrote another letter in code, this one to General Wilkinson, who was leaving Natchez that same day, going into the field. This document, undoubtedly the most remarkable ever penned by Aaron Burr, is reproduced in its entirety:

> Your letter postmarked May 13th is received. I, Aaron Burr, have obtained funds and have actually commenced the enterprise. Detachments from different points and under

various pretensions will rendezvous on the Ohio, 1st of November.

Everything internal and external favors views.

Naval protection of England is assured. Truxton is going to Jamaica to arrange with the admiral on that station. It will meet us at the Mississippi. England, a navy of the United States, are ready to join, and final orders are given to my friends and followers.

It will be a host of choice spirits. Wilkinson shall be second to Burr only; Wilkinson shall dictate the rank and promotion of his officers.

Burr has gone westward, 1st August, never to return. With him goes his daughter; her husband will follow in October with a corps of worthies.

Send forthwith an intelligent and confidential friend with whom Burr may confer; he shall return immediately with further interesting details; this is essential to concert and harmony of movement. Send a list of all persons to Wilkinson west of the mountains who could be useful, with a note delineating their character. By your messenger send me four or five commissions of your officers, which you can borrow on any pretext you please; they shall be turned faithfully.

Already are orders given to the contractor to forward provisions to points Wilkinson may name; this shall not be used until the last moment and then under proper injunctions.

The object is brought to the point so long desired. Burr guarantees the result with his life and honor, with the lives and honor and fortunes of hundreds of the best blood of the country. Burr's plan of operation is to move down rapidly from the Falls on the 15th of November with the first five hundred to one thousand men, in light boats now constructed for that purpose; to be at Natchez between the 5th and 15th of December, there to meet you, there to determine whether it will be expedient in the first instance to seize on or pass by Baton Rouge.

On receipt of this send Baton Rouge.

Draw on Burr for all expenses, etc.

The people of the country to which we are going are prepared to receive us; their agents, now with Burr, say that if we will protect their religion, and not subject them to a foreign power, that in three weeks all will be settled.

The gods invite us to glory and fortune; it remains to be seen whether we deserve the boon.

The bearer of this goes express to you. He is a man of inviolable honor, and perfect discretion, formed to execute rather than project, capable of relating facts with fidelity, and incapable of relating them otherwise; he is thoroughly informed of the plans and intentions of Burr, and will disclose to you as far as you inquire and no further. He has imbibed a reverence for your character, and may be embarrassed in your presence; put him at ease, and he will satisfy you.

The freely mixed fact and fancy in this communication to Wilkinson is readily apparent. All of his statements regarding naval arrangements were the products of his inspired imagination and had literally no basis in truth. Great Britain had made no agreement with him and knew nothing specific regarding his venture. Commodore Truxton was not a party to the conspiracy and was making no trip to the headquarters of the Royal Navy's Caribbean Squadron at Jamaica; the plan for the meeting of that squadron and Colonel Burr at the mouth of the Mississippi existed only in Burr's mind.

It was true that he himself was on the march, accompanied by his daughter and a corps of men, but he neglected to say that the vast majority of his troops believed they were taking part in a campaign on behalf of the United States. He also failed to indicate that the five hundred to one thousand men comprised his entire corps; his tricky wording hinted that his entire force was much larger, which was decidedly not the case.

Wilkinson was stunned by the letter. Until that time he had halfheartedly played along with Burr, never quite allowing himself to believe that the conspiracy would materialize. He lacked faith in the overall scheme, as well as in the generalship of the future emperor, and he saw gaping holes in the structural pattern of the plan that Aaron, blinded by his own optimism, could not visualize. The general, knew he was already partially compromised, although he had thus far committed no overt act of treason. What made him uneasiest was Burr's unexplained request for the loan of four or five of his officers' commissions. What did Burr intend to do with these documents? Wilkinson had no idea but realized the purpose was necessarily nefarious and would drag him even deeper into the mire of conspiracy.

Nineteenth-century historians related that James Wilkinson became panicky, but they may have been influenced by their own prejudices and emotions. His actions, taken immediately after receipt of the letter, indicate that a cool mind was at work and that he was determined to clear himself at any cost, including the sacrifice of Aaron Burr.

Wilkinson spent the better part of the night of October 8 at his St. Louis headquarters deciphering the letter, and the following morning he summoned his deputy, a Colonel Cushing, to a breakfast conference. First he asked whether the colonel was aware of a Burr conspiracy. When the deputy indicated ignorance, Wilkinson informed him there was, indeed, such a conspiracy. Burr's messenger, Samuel Swartwout, of New York, one of his closest cronies, was called in and asked for additional information.

Swartwout, a man of limited intelligence whose loyalty to Aaron Burr was absolute, had no way of knowing that Wilkinson was in the process of turning on his master for the sake of saving his own skin. He had been instructed to reveal anything the general asked, and he obeyed Burr's orders to the letter. Colonel Burr, he said, had evolved the most clever plan in history. When he reached New Orleans, he would seize control of the government there. Then he would commandeer all ships in the city's harbor, borrow the gold bullion in the New Orleans bank vaults, and after asking for additional volunteers, sail for Vera Cruz. He expected to capture the principal Mexican port without a struggle and thereafter would march on Mexico City. He was no longer satisfied with the idea of capturing a mere portion of Mexican domain but intended to add all Mexico to his empire.

While the astonished Colonel Cushing tried to grasp the enormity of all he had heard, Wilkinson permitted Swartwout to return to his master. Thereafter, conferring again with his deputy, he outlined a new plan to meet the emergency. Spain had long kept a few scattered battalions on the west bank of the Mississippi River to guard her borders. Now, with the increase in bad feeling due to the territorial ambitions of Americans who wanted to move farther westward, Spain had increased her patrols, and it appeared as if a border conflict, although probably not a full-scale war, was imminent. Wilkinson decided to arrange a truce with the Spaniards across the river so he could devote his full attention to the capture of Aaron Burr and the dismemberment of his irregular corps. Putting the plan into immediate action, he approached the Spaniards under a white flag, and the truce was arranged without difficulty.

On October 10 Wilkinson dispatched two brief letters. The shorter of them was addressed to the Spanish viceroy for all of the New World, who made his headquarters in Mexico City. In return for a prompt payment of $150,000 in gold, he declared, he would reveal the details of a horrendous plot against Spanish interests in North America.

The second, somewhat longer communication was addressed to President Jefferson. In short, blunt sentences Wilkinson outlined the major points of the Burr conspiracy, then indicated that he was taking the steps necessary to secure the interests of the United States. He also urgently requested further instructions.

The letter was curious in one respect: Wilkinson did not name the principal member of the plot, claiming he did not know the man's identity. He pretended he had learned the details but had not yet succeeded in unearthing the identity of the prime mover. In making this maneuver the general outsmarted himself, since intelligent men leaped to inevitable conclusions and implicated him in the conspiracy, too.

Thomas Jefferson received the communication on November 25 and was neither surprised nor shocked. For many weeks he had been hearing rumors and received warnings about Aaron Burr's activities from men of prominence in Pennsylvania, Ohio, Kentucky, and Tennessee. The army's Commander-in-Chief, who was also the United States Governor of Upper Louisiana, had not named the head of the conspiracy, but Jefferson accurately concluded that it was Aaron Burr. The President called in Secretary of State Madison, Burr's longtime friend, and showed him the evidence. Madison was saddened and was forced to agree that the man who had been his friend since their college days had to be taken into custody.

He also agreed with the President's plan: Jefferson intended to issue a proclamation in which he would declare a state of emergency because of the existence of a plot to dismember the West. He would also order that all participants in the conspiracy be placed under arrest. But he, like Wilkinson, did not mention Aaron Burr by name. Remembering how the wily Burr had avoided apprehension by the authorities of New York and New Jersey, he preferred to match cleverness with cleverness. Rather than alarming the culprit, the President left a deliberate loophole in his proclamation. If the perpetrator of the scheme lived up to his past record, he would not flee but would brazenly remain within American jurisdiction and consequently would be that much easier to apprehend.

While these dramatic events were taking place, Burr was encountering more than his share of troubles and had been compelled to spend the entire autumn in Kentucky and Tennessee. On three different occasions he was called into the United States Courthouse in Frankfort, Kentucky, to answer charges made by District Attorney Joseph H. Daviess to the effect that he was "guilty of conduct injurious to the interests of the United States." Daviess had heard rumors but was unable to prove them, and on all three occasions the court allowed Burr to go free.

In mid-October Burr also learned that the people of Ohio had turned against him. So many stories were being told about the men drilling in secret on Blennerhassett's island that the militia was planning to move in, confiscate the stores of provisions and arms, and disperse the "troops" in training there. Burr proposed that he himself return to straighten out the situation but was told in so many words that the militia considered him a traitor and would shoot him on sight, giving him no opportunity to offer an explanation.

These problems were relatively minor; the most serious was a collusion with the indomitable and patriotic General Andrew Jackson, of Tennessee. As the autumn had progressed and additional recruits had flocked to Burr's banner, he had found it necessary to increase his order for flat-boats, munitions, and food supplies. These could not be procured overnight for him, but Jackson, aided by his close friend, Colonel John Coffee, had been working diligently to obtain all that the genial "General" Burr wanted. Then, thanks to the indiscretion of a Burr confederate, Jackson learned the basic outlines of the conspiracy.

This man, a Captain Fort, arrived in Nashville on December 15 and was received so cordially by Jackson and Coffee that he leaped to the false conclusion they were also privy to the plot. Under adroit questioning he revealed that "General" Burr planned to seize New Orleans, take possession of all the Louisiana Territory, and after quickly conquering Mexico, add the American land to his new empire.

On December 17 Burr arrived to take possession of his flatboats and supplies but instead was confronted by a grim Andrew Jackson and an equally outraged John Coffee. Few men managed to survive one of Andrew Jackson's verbal barrages, and under ordinary circumstances Burr would have challenged him to a duel, which would have been interesting, since Jackson's markmanship may have been equal to his own. But this was no time for personal vendettas; too much depended on Jackson's goodwill and cooperation.

Never had Aaron Burr been in such a tight spot, and never before had he talked with such earnest conviction. He vehemently denied everything Captain Fort had said, swore he was a loyal citizen of the United States, and as a final argument, produced a new, conveniently forged document. This was a supposed order from President Jefferson, directing him to declare martial law in New Orleans, take command of the city as military government, and use it as the base of his operations against Mexico.

Jackson and Coffee were still suspicious but lacked any concrete evidence against Burr. Reluctant to act without proof against the former Vice-President of the United States, Jackson allowed him to depart, taking two of the completed barges and large quantities of supplies. Burr had escaped one major pitfall but would soon learn that his troubles were just beginning.

Chapter 15

One basic flaw in the grand design of Aaron Burr's conspiracy was simple: Too many people knew too much about it. The fault for this state of affairs rested with Burr. His vanity, combined with his self-confidence and his ambition, led him to confuse his dreams with reality. He was so eager to share the dazzling product of his imagination with his followers that he divulged details that a more prudent man would have confided to no one but a small handful of trusted lieutenants. That was not Burr's way of doing things, however, and his verbal indiscretion was one of the principal causes of his downfall.

For months there had been talk about the activities on Blennerhassett's island, and the rumors had been so insistent that it finally became impossible for the authorities to ignore them. Ohio and Virginia worked out a joint plan and acted in concert.

On December 19, while Burr was in the process of leaving Nashville with two barges and a fraction of the supplies that Andrew Jackson had accumulated for him, the Ohio militia struck. A flotilla of barges and canoes had left Blennerhassett's island the previous day, and a trap was set at Marietta, on the Ohio River. Fourteen boats were captured, and more than two hundred barrels of gunpowder and provisions were seized. Approximately 100 men were arrested and subsequently released because there was insufficient evidence against them to prosecute, while another 150 escaped into the nearby woods and scattered.

On December 20, when news of the catastrophe reached the island, a messenger brought word that the Virginia militia would conduct a raid that night. Blennerhassett fled with about fifty men, and so great was his haste that he left his wife and about fifteen of his followers behind. The report he received was correct. The Virginia militia did arrive that night and promptly treated his property as booty. The contents of his wine cellar disappeared, valuable bric-a-brac vanished, and some of his expensive imported furniture was used as firewood.

Blennerhassett and his companions continued their voyage down the Ohio, the decimated band eluding the militiamen who were searching for them.

Burr sailed his two rafts down the Cumberland River toward its junction with the Ohio, confidently expecting to meet his entire force under Blennerhassett's command. At some time during his voyage his path crossed that of the messenger bearing President Jefferson's proclamation, which ordered the arrest of those who were conspiring against the United States.

No details of this meeting are known, but posterity has accepted the story that the presidential courier failed to realize that Aaron Burr was the leader of the treasonable movement and innocently showed him the proclamation. According to another, less likely account, Burr concealed his identity from the messenger and in this way was able to peruse the document. Whatever may have transpired, Burr realized that the essence of his plan was known to Washington City. Soon Andrew Jackson would read the presidential order, and the instant he realized he had been duped, he would organize the Tennessee militia for a pursuit of the escaping would-be emperor of the West.

Burr realized that the odds against him were mounting rapidly, but even now he did not give in to despair. Incredible though it may appear to later generations, he clung to the hope that he could still bring off his coup. He had an ample head start on General Jackson and the Tennessee militia, and he knew it would take time to organize a chase. Also, he had no idea that James Wilkinson had abandoned him, so he still believed he could take possession of New Orleans, seize the gold and shipping there, and set out for Vera Cruz, precisely as he had planned.

On December 23 he met Blennerhassett at the appointed rendezvous — the confluence of the Cumberland and Ohio rivers — and was stunned to hear of the heavy losses he had suffered. But this blow, like those that had preceded it, did not deter him. Although his total band numbered fewer than seventy-five men, he pushed on, his insolence undiminished. On Christmas Day he sent a messenger ahead to Fort Massac, offering the commandant the "compliments of the season," and four days later he made his overnight camp only one mile from the fort.

The commandant, a Captain Bissell, graciously invited him to dine at the fort, and Burr, equally gracious, declined with thanks. He had no intention of being trapped in a compound of the United States Army in the event that Bissell already knew of his conspiracy or learned of it while he was there.

On the last day of 1806 the little flotilla moved into the broad waters of the Mississippi River from the Ohio, and on January 1, 1807, forty recruits joined the company at the town of New Madrid. Three days later Aaron called a halt at Chickasaw Bluff, later Memphis, where a small army garrison was located. There he perpetrated his most audacious act, winning the commandant, Lieutenant Jacob Jackson, a measure of dubious immortality.

Producing his forged commission from the President, Burr ordered the lieutenant to raise a troop of volunteers without delay, follow him to New Orleans within forty-eight hours, and accompany him on an expedition to Mexico! The unknowing young officer not only did his best to comply with the command of "General" Burr, but actually enlisted his entire garrison for the campaign. Forty-eight hours was too short a time to ready the volunteers, and a few days later when the men were ready to leave, there had been a drastic change in the situation.

The troops stationed at Chickasaw Bluff took no part in the adventure for the simple reason that Burr's luck now began to run out. On January 8 the little flotilla reached Natchez, but Burr did not go ashore there. This caused the first ground swell of unrest in his company. A good meal awaited the men in the town, where they could also find liquor and women, and they could not understand why their leader had refused their request to make an overnight halt there.

Burr continued to sail down the Mississippi until he reached Bayou Pierre, about thirty miles above New Orleans, where he went ashore at the home of a friend named Bruin, from whom he hoped to learn the latest developments. Bruin showed him the New Orleans newspapers, and two articles met Burr's startled gaze. The first was the reproduction of a long letter that began: "I, Aaron Burr, have obtained funds and have actually commenced the enterprise."

Burr instantly sensed that Wilkinson either had betrayed him or had himself been captured. But it was the second piece he saw in the newspapers that made his blood run cold. He read the heavy print with a heart equally heavy:

REWARD TWO THOUSAND DOLLARS — REWARD
FOR THE CAPTURE AND ARREST OF COLONEL
AARON BURR FORMER VICE-PRESIDENT OF THE
UNITED STATES OF AMERICA

At that moment Aaron Burr's wild dream evaporated. He was now a criminal, a fugitive from justice, wanted by the government of the United States for treason and conspiracy.

It was too late to escape. Word of his coming had preceded him to New Orleans, and a fleet of Louisiana Territory gunboats was moving up the river to capture him. His vessels were surrounded, and he was taken into custody by United States marshals, assisted by a platoon of soldiers. Always the gentleman, Burr surrendered with good grace.

A grand jury was convened at Bayou Pierre, and Burr represented himself. Never before had he spoken with such conviction to a jury; never before had he displayed such sincerity. He and his companions, he insisted, were immigrants who intended to settle on lands to which he had a claim, and he produced documents for the jury's inspection. The charges of treason and conspiracy were absurd, since he had no arms or gunpowder on board his rafts. What actually happened to this evidence is not known, but several of Burr's subordinates indicated, at a much later date, that he had heaved them overboard a few moments before the gunboats had closed in on his rafts.

Still a gallant leader, Burr posted a bond of five thousand dollars in cash for his bewildered followers prior to their own grand-jury hearing. He also insisted they were completely innocent of wrongdoing, which was more or less the truth. In all, his conduct was so exemplary that the jury set him free.

The federal authorities had anticipated precisely such a move. Familiar with Burr's sway over juries, they were ready to pounce a second time, and before he could leave the little frame courthouse at Bayou Pierre, they placed him under arrest again, informing him that he would be tried before a court-martial board.

Burr realized he was trapped and that Wilkinson was responsible. Because of his own vulnerability, the guilty Wilkinson had chosen the one way to clear his own name. A court-martial board consisting of senior officers friendly to their superior would condemn Aaron Burr to death, and he would be shot before he could reveal that General Wilkinson had been his partner in treason. Eloquent appeals would not be effective, nor would knowledge of the law. It didn't matter, in fact, that a trial by a court-martial board was a legally questionable procedure; he would be dead before the matter could be raised in the civilian courts, and there were few Americans who would mourn the execution of a traitor.

Burr saw only one chance and seized it. Rather than protest against a trial by court-martial, he insisted on his right to prepare a defense. The American sense of fair play would have been outraged had he been denied this opportunity, so the army reluctantly released him on bail, several New Orleans friends putting up the necessary five thousand dollars for the purpose.

Burr had no intention of standing trial in a court under General Wilkinson's jurisdiction and immediately disappeared. His precise whereabouts from January 31 to February 13, 1807, have never been determined, and only a few facts are known. In some unexplained manner he obtained a horse, frontiersman's clothing, a blanket, cooking utensils, and a supply of food. Then he vanished into the jungles of the lower Louisiana Territory. It is possible, even probable, that he crossed the Mississippi River, hoping to reach a settlement in New Spain where he could tell a story that would win him refuge. If this was his intention, he was doomed to disappointment. The Marquis de Casa Yrujo shared the indignation of President Jefferson, and Spanish troops in the wilderness west of the Mississippi had received standing instructions to apprehend the fugitive if he came within their grasp.

Perhaps, during his flight, Burr saw one or more Spanish patrols and realized that the Spaniards would deal harshly with him. That is the only logical explanation for his abrupt return to American soil; he had more room to maneuver in American courts than he would if forced to face the uncompromising bar of Spanish justice.

Exceptionally heavy rains had forced both the Americans and the Spaniards to abandon their manhunt. General Wilkinson issued an order in which he assumed that the fugitive would try to make his way to the Floridas in the hope that he could find a merchant brig willing to give him passage to Great Britain or France, either of which nation would have given him refuge.

If Burr had entertained any such plan of escape, however, he abandoned it because the risks were too great. Instead he returned to the Louisiana Territory and banked on the hope that he would not be recognized.

Shortly before sundown on February 13 two men were sitting in a little tavern on the one street of a small Louisiana Territory town called Wakefield, chatting and drinking ale. A stranger appeared at the door to ask about the location of the road leading to the East, and one of the pair gave him directions. The other, a country lawyer named Nicholas Perkins, studied the stranger, who was attired in the faded leather trousers and shirt of the frontier, with a poncho slung over his shoulder, and on his face was a two-week growth of beard. At first glance he looked like any one of hundreds in the area.

But two things caught Perkins's notice. The man was wearing the sharply pointed boots of an aristocrat, boots that obviously had been made to his order. Studying him more closely, Perkins was struck by the magnetic, almost feverish quality of the man's eyes. About thirty minutes after the stranger's departure Perkins leaped to his feet. He had read the details of the notice offering a reward for the capture of Aaron Burr, and the circular had stressed the quality of his eyes.

Perkins hurried to nearby Fort Stoddart, a wilderness outpost, and the commandant, a Lieutenant Gaines, set out at once with a detachment of cavalry. The following day, in midmorning, the column overtook a battered figure, riding alone. According to the report Gaines submitted to General Wilkinson, a brief discussion took place.

"I presume, sir, that I have the honor of addressing Colonel Burr," the lieutenant said.

Burr remained brazen. "I do not recognize your right to ask such a question," he replied.

"I arrest you at the instance of the federal government," the lieutenant said.

The fugitive was taken into custody but did not give up his struggle. He tried every maneuver at his command, threatening to bring legal action against Lieutenant Gaines for false arrest, pleading for compassion on the grounds that he was the victim of unwarranted persecution, and haughtily demanding that he be released on bail. None of his stratagems succeeded, and he was taken to Fort Stoddart under heavy escort.

There were no facilities for housing a distinguished prisoner at the fort, so Burr was taken into Gaines's own home, where he lived more as a guest than as an escaped criminal who had finally been caught. Gaines's brother was ill, and Burr looked after him, prescribing medication that was effective and thereby winning the young man's gratitude. He taught Mrs. Gaines a number of recipes, discussed literature with her, and in the evenings played chess with her. He also had long talks with the sentries posted outside the house to prevent him from escaping again and completely charmed these soldiers.

The lieutenant, in a report to General Wilkinson, said that if he had been forced to keep the prisoner in his custody for as long as an additional week, the consequences would have been serious. It appears that the former Vice-President almost charmed his way to freedom.

Lawyer Nicholas Perkins, however, was determined to win the reward of two thousand dollars, and this obscure, hard-nosed frontier dweller became Aaron Burr's nemesis. At his insistence a strong cavalry escort was provided by Lieutenant Gaines, and Perkins personally accompanied the party on the ride East, intending to deliver the prisoner to President Jefferson himself so they could claim the reward without delay.

Burr remained in seemingly good spirits during the journey and showed no resentment toward Perkins, who kept a continuous, day-and-night watch over him. The prisoner's good humor won him the admiration of the soldiers who comprised his guard, and they were particularly impressed by the fact that he made no attempt to escape.

Burr had made his plans with care and waited until the party reached the sympathetic southern states on the Atlantic seaboard. South Carolina was the home of the influential Alston family, and since Theodosia had returned to her husband, he was certain his son-in-law would help him. As the little caravan halted one morning in the center of a small South Carolina town, the prisoner jumped to the ground, announced his identity, and shouting loudly, demanded civilian protection.

Before the startled citizens could react, Nicholas Perkins ordered the captive surrounded, then demanded that Colonel Burr remount.

Burr refused.

The exasperated Perkins picked him up, deposited him in the saddle, and ordered the escort to resume the march. Burr had suffered the ultimate public ignominy.

Chapter 16

The trial of Aaron Burr on charges of treason against the United States of America was the greatest spectacle the new Republic had ever witnessed. The central figure, of course, was the former Vice-President, but President Jefferson had brought the charges, so his own prestige was at stake. The presiding judge was Chief Justice John Marshall, the first jurist of the land, which added to the excitement.

According to the custom of the time, only Justice Marshall, rather than the entire Supreme Court, was on the bench. No facilities suitable for the solemn trial were available in Washington City, so the House of Burgesses in Richmond, Virginia, was used. Hundreds of people, including United States senators and representatives, foreign diplomats, and high-ranking army officers were in attendance, as were ordinary citizens who hoped to find seats in the public galleries.

The crowds began to gather in mid-May, and a distinct air of uneasiness was noted in the ranks of President Jefferson's loyal followers. The reason for their restlessness was not difficult to understand: Chief Justice Marshall had already tried Burr's principal messengers, Samuel Swartwout and Erich Bollmann, on charges of treason and had found both men innocent. Marshall had been emphatic when he had declared that the Constitution defined treason as "an overt act of levying war" against the United States, and he had found the actions of neither messenger treasonable. Aaron Burr's now-famous coded letter to General Wilkinson had been introduced as evidence against the defendants, but the Chief Justice had made it clear that in his opinion the document said nothing that could be interpreted as a plan to seize or otherwise acquire territory belonging to the United States.

The Chief Justice's interpretation was unnerving, and Secretary of State Madison privately agreed with Secretary of the Treasury Gallatin, who predicted that after the dust of scandal cleared away, the renowned defendant would be acquitted. The strong-willed President Jefferson let it be known he would be satisfied with nothing less than a finding of guilty. For posterity's sake he hoped that Burr and his principal accomplices would be hanged; such an act would discourage treason in the future.

John Marshall was as strong-willed as the President and believed that the Constitution itself was on trial. If the judicial branch of the government was to win universal recognition as being the equal of the executive and legislative branches, the desires of the President in this case were irrelevant, and the judicial alone would determine the guilt or innocence of the defendant.

Relations between the President and the Chief Justice were already strained because Marshall, acting against Jefferson's express wishes, had ordered the defendant freed on bail at a preliminary hearing held in March, soon after Burr reached Washington City. Jefferson believed that a man who had tried to escape well might make another attempt, but Marshall had paid no attention to the President's views.

The legal talent assembled by both sides was formidable. At the President's personal order the chief prosecutor was United States District Attorney George Hay, considered by many to be the most brilliant trial lawyer in the country. Associated with him were Alexander McRae and William Wirt, both of whom were prominent in the government, plus a battery of a half-dozen assistants. Aaron Burr's principal attorney was Luther Martin, of Maryland, an eccentric genius whose courtroom oratory could be matched by no one in the United States with the possible exception of Aaron Burr himself. Associated with Martin were three senior advisers: Charles Lee, the noted Edmund Randolph, and John Wickham — all of them men who had long distinguished themselves at the bar. Acting as associates were two much younger men — John Baker and Benjamin Botts — noted for their ability to sway juries.

According to Washington Irving, who attended the trial as a reporter for a number of newspapers that had banded together to hire him for that purpose, the real principal attorney for the defense was Colonel Aaron Burr himself. He presided at the long strategy meetings held in the days prior to the opening of the trial, and it was he who planned the major outlines of the defense.

That strategy became clear on May 22, 1807, the opening day of the trial, when Burr personally rose to challenge the seating of two members of the grand jury — Senator William B. Giles and Congressman Wilson Nicholas, both of whom were staunch Republican-Democratic supporters of the President. Under Burr's adroit questioning both men admitted they had already formed opinions in the case, and the Chief Justice promptly dismissed them. The defense had attacked first and had drawn blood.

District Attorney Hay realized from the outset that the defense was appealing over the heads of the Chief Justice and the grand jury to the American public at large. This, he wrote Jefferson in a confidential memorandum, compounded the difficulties facing the prosecution, but he promised to deal with the situation to the best of his ability.

From the beginning of the trial Aaron Burr appeared completely self-confident, and Washington Irving described his manner as jaunty. There was good reason for his optimism. Neither British Minister Anthony Merry nor Spanish Minister de Casa Yrujo had come forward to volunteer his services as a witness for the simple reason that neither wanted to make it known that he had treated with the defendant or urged his government to support him. Therefore, the acts of actual, overt treason Burr had committed when he dealt with the foreign envoys were unknown to the prosecution.

He realized, too, that his principal assistants, among them Dayton and Blennerhassett, could not give evidence against him without implicating themselves. Consequently he felt certain they would remain loyal.

Other witnesses, including Andrew Jackson and John Coffee, of Tennessee, could present only hearsay evidence that was immediately ruled invalid. In fact, General Jackson was known to believe the President was a coward in his dealings with foreign powers, so the prosecution was reluctant to call him to the stand. Such minor figures as Commodore Truxton and "General" William Eaton became confused under defense cross-questioning, so their testimony was of little value.

As the outlines of the alleged plot against the United States were drawn and filled in, it became clear to the prosecution and defense alike that Aaron Burr's fate would rest on the testimony of Brigadier General James Wilkinson, Commander-in-Chief of the Army and Federal Governor of the Upper Louisiana Territory. Wilkinson had been issued a subpoena but had not yet come to Richmond from his headquarters in the West.

The prosecution made no secret of its belief that Wilkinson's testimony would send Burr to the gallows, and according to

Washington Irving, betting men were wagering that the defendant would vanish the very day that Wilkinson arrived in town. District Attorney Hay shared that opinion and begged the court to imprison the defendant. The Chief Justice refused, but Hay's pleas were so eloquent that Marshall increased Burr's bail from ten thousand dollars to twenty thousand.

All through the trial Burr was the model of a dapper, debonair gentleman. His conduct in the courtroom was decorous, and he could be seen any afternoon in a Richmond tavern, sipping a mild glass of sack as he discussed the case with his battery of attorneys. His lovely daughter and her small child came to Richmond, and he won the sympathy of the city's matrons by taking a daily carriage ride with his grandson.

The delay in the appearance of General Wilkinson gave the defense an opportunity to launch a major counterattack, and Burr himself has been credited with thinking of the device. The court was startled one morning when Colonel Burr stood and requested that a subpoena be issued to the President of the United States.

The stunned prosecution demanded to know the reason for this unprecedented request.

Principal defense attorney Luther Martin replied in a statement that gave the case a new significance. Aaron Burr was being tried, he said in effect, not because of alleged treason he had committed, but because he was the political opponent of the President.

The prosecution protested vigorously.

But neither Hay nor any member of his team was a match for Luther Martin, who struck sparks of verbal lightning when he said:

This is a peculiar case, Mr. Justice.

The President has undertaken to prejudice my client by declaring that "Of his guilt there can be no doubt." He has assumed to himself the knowledge of the Supreme Being Himself, and has pretended to search the heart of my highly respected friend. He has proclaimed him a traitor in the face of that country which has rewarded him. He has let slip the dogs of war, the hell hounds of persecution to hunt down my noble, innocent friend.

And would this President of the United States, who has raised all this absurd clamor, pretend to keep the papers which are wanted for this trial where life itself is at stake?

It is a sacred principle that in all such cases the accused has a right to all the evidence which is necessary for his defense. And whoever withholds, willfully, information that would save the life of a person charged with a capital offence is substantially a murderer, and so recorded in the register of heaven.

What, sir, shall the Cabinet of the United States be converted into a lion's mouth of Venice or a *repertorium* of the bloody Inquisition? Shall envy, hatred and all the malignant passions pour their poison into that Cabinet against the character and life of a fellow citizen?

We are told that we ought to respect the President. Will the President this himself insulted by the demand of a mere document?

Mr. Justice, we appeal to the Supreme Maker that we only wish justice and fear only perjury. We approach with uplifted hands the sacred altar of justice as a sanctuary to screen us, not from just punishment, but from unjust rancorous persecution! From this sanctuary we confidently expect protection!

The uproar in the House of Burgesses was so great that it was impossible for the bailiffs to restore order, and the Chief Justice was compelled to adjourn court for the day.

The arguments were resumed the following morning, and it became clear that the defense was adamant in its desire to subpoena President Jefferson because he had been the recipient of the letter from General Wilkinson that had been responsible for the presidential proclamation resulting in Aaron Burr's arrest. The defense demanded the right to question Jefferson about that communication and insisted that Jefferson be compelled to produce it in court.

The prosecution replied with the argument that Thomas Jefferson had been the recipient of the letter in his capacity as President and that any letter addressed to the Chief Executive of the United States was privileged. The defense countered with the statement that the so-called rights of executive privilege, which were nowhere mentioned in the Constitution, could send an innocent man to his death. The fight raged for four days, and the Chief Justice, recognizing the constitutional significance of the debate, made no attempt to cut it short. The more the prosecution stressed the prerogatives of the Presidency, the more virulent became the attack of the defense on the man who held the nation's highest office.

Jefferson, who received daily reports on the progress of the battle, realized that Aaron Burr was making a successful attempt to unite his political foes. The newspapers faithfully revealed every line of important dialogue in the courtroom, and men in every state who were opposed to the policies of the administration lined up in support of the beleaguered Aaron Burr. The President knew the defense was shifting the very nature of the case from one sphere to another, but he was powerless to halt the trend.

At the end of the fourth day of debate Chief Justice Marshall ordered an adjournment until noon of the following day, at which time he promised to render a decision. The House of

Burgesses was hushed the next day at noon when the Chief Justice announced that he was issuing a subpoena commanding the President's appearance.

The document was duly served, but Thomas Jefferson was aware not only of the present situation, but of precedent. Therefore he chose to ignore the summons. The court was powerless to force him to appear, but it became obvious that his refusal dealt a severe blow to the prosecution's hopes.

On June 23, one month after the beginning of the trial, at a time when the prosecution was afraid the case would be dismissed because of a lack of evidence against the defendant, Brigadier General James Wilkinson arrived in Richmond, riding into town in his full-dress uniform. The next day he appeared in court and took the stand to tell his story. He testified all day and coolly avoided the many traps set for him by the counsel for the defense, knowing it would be necessary for Burr to admit his own guilt if he expected to catch his former colleague, too. The most damaging statement the defense could wring from him was the admission that he had slightly altered the text of Aaron's letter to him before releasing it to the press.

On June 25 the prosecution and the counsel for the defense presented long-winded summations of their respective positions to the grand jury. Colonel Burr's demeanor was unchanged, Washington Irving wrote, and his face remained calm.

The next morning the grand jury retired to begin its deliberations, which continued all that day and the next. Late in the afternoon of June 27 they returned to the chamber of the Burgesses, and the foreman announced their verdict. They found Aaron Burr guilty and recommended that he be indicted for treason and misdemeanor.

The defendant smiled slightly but remained composed, Irving wrote. The prosecution immediately demanded that the defendant's bail be canceled and that he be confined to a penitentiary for safekeeping. The court ruled, however, that inasmuch as Colonel Burr had made no attempt to violate his parole while on bail, the present arrangement would remain unchanged. The prosecution appealed the decision, and the Chief Justice reluctantly changed his opinion and ordered the defendant confined in a "suite in the Richmond penitentiary."

At least a score of Richmond's most prominent citizens acted as an escort of honor as Aaron Burr was taken to the prison. There his "suite" soon became transformed into a salon. Theodosia spent the better part of each day with her father, ladies of the city vied with each other for the right to provide his meals, and other sympathetic friends made certain that he lacked no luxury. Burr languished in the penitentiary for a full month while the court was in recess, but aside from the humiliation of imprisonment, he suffered no lack of the good things in life that had long been important to him.

Every day throughout the month of July he conferred with his attorneys, and he shared their conviction that his prospects were grim. Under the rules of a cumbersome judicial system he was, in effect, being tried twice for the same crime and having been indicted by the grand jury, now would actually be tried for treason. He and his lawyers had fired every cannon in their arsenal, but the grand jury's verdict of guilty was a damaging blow that would be difficult, if not impossible, to counteract.

Never in his fifty-one years had Burr demonstrated cowardice in the face of the enemy, and he did not flinch in his hour of supreme crisis. His courage unflagging, his mind keen, and his sense of humor undiminished, he directed his lawyers in the preparation of his penultimate defense, consistently stressing that he had committed no *overt* act of treason.

Chapter 17

For all practical purposes the grand-jury investigation of Aaron Burr had been a trial, so the actual trial, which opened on August 3, 1807, would have been anticlimactic had it not been for the indisputable fact that the life of one of the most prominent citizens of the United States was at stake. The public was still absorbed, officials of the federal and state governments could talk of little else, and foreign nations sent observers to sit in the courtroom, the principal chamber of the Virginia House of Burgesses in Richmond. The summer was the warmest Virginia had known in years, the courtroom was stifling, and even the most decorous of the attorneys on both sides informally obtained the permission of Chief Justice Marshall to appear without the heavy wigs that were considered an integral part of a lawyer's courtroom costume.

Aaron Burr had his counsel served notice from the outset that they intended to fight to the last. The grand jury's verdict had been a nasty blow, but the defense had no intention of abandoning hope. Every prospective juror was examined with infinite care and cross-questioned on the stand, and the twelve men who were ultimately selected were forced to run a legal gauntlet that to the best of human ability, insured they entertained no prejudices against Aaron Burr.

The principal hopes of the defense rested on the constitutional interpretation of treason and the validation of its commission. Not only was it necessary for a man to have committed an overt act for him to be judged guilty, but that act had to be proved by the sworn testimony of two witnesses.

Burr felt certain it would be difficult, perhaps impossible, for the prosecution to provide two such witnesses to his defection.

District Attorney George Hay fired the opening salvo for the prosecution, saying he intended to prove Burr's treason in accordance with the Chief Justice's own interpretation in the Swartwout-Bollmann case: "If a body of men be actually assembled for a treasonable purpose; all who perform any part, however minute, or however remote from the scene of action are traitors." Armed men had gathered on Blennerhassett's island for the purpose of committing treason, Hay said, and although Colonel Burr had been in Kentucky and Tennessee at the time, he was the true instigator of the mutiny.

The first witness called by the prosecution was "General" William Eaton. Burr leaped to his feet, objecting because, he said, any testimony given by Eaton would necessarily refer to conversations that had taken place in Washington City. The court ruled that Eaton could take the stand.

Conscious of the fact that the entire nation was listening, the egocentric Eaton thoroughly enjoyed his day in court. In a long, rambling recital, which the prosecution made no attempt to curb, he recounted his own exploits against the pirate monarchs of the Barbary Coast of North Africa. He made it plain that he resented the refusal of President Jefferson to recognize his exploits, and the defense became aware of the prosecution's cleverness. Eaton's testimony against Aaron Burr would be all the more valuable because the jury was now informed that he was no friend of the President.

After spending the entire morning on the stand, Eaton returned after the noon recess to describe, in detail, his conversations in Washington City with Colonel Burr. His evidence was damning, but Aaron Burr was still more than a match for opposition attorneys. Eaton's claims against the government had been settled a short time earlier, and the "general" had received a payment in the amount of ten thousand dollars. That fact was brought out by Burr himself in cross-questioning, and he went on, with infinite skill and patience, to force the witness to admit he had agreed to testify in the treason case *after* he had received his money.

The implications were obvious. Without making the charge in so many words, Burr managed to indicate that Eaton and the federal government had made an under-the-table deal. The hero of the North African campaign had been paid his claim in full and in return had become a prosecution witness. Thus Eaton's testimony was completely discredited in the eyes of the jury, and the defense won its first victory.

Commodore Thomas Truxton was the next witness, and his evidence was damning, too, until Burr personally cross-examined him. A portion of that cross-examination shows how adroit Burr could be when cornered:

> BURR: Did you ever hear me express any intention or sentiment respecting a division of the Union?
> TRUXTON: No, sir. I never heard you express such intentions or sentiments.
> BURR: Did I not state to you that the Mexican expedition would be very beneficial to the United States?
> TRUXTON: You did.
> BURR: Had you any serious doubt as to my intention to settle those lands [the proposed colony in the Louisiana Territory]?
> TRUXTON: Far from that.
> JURY FOREMAN: Was the expedition against Mexico to take place only in the event of a war between the United States and Spain?
> BURR: In other words, Commodore, my expedition would not have initiated such a war, but would have invaded

Mexico only in the event that a state of war with Spain already existed; that is to say, in the event that General Wilkinson's army and the armies of Spain engaged in conflict, only then would I have led my expedition into Mexico.

TRUXTON: That was my clear understanding of your intentions, Colonel Burr.

BURR: Did I indicate to you that it was my intention to keep any portion of Mexican territory for myself?

TRUXTON: No.

BURR: It is my intention, then, as expressed to you, to plant the flag of the United States in these lands?

TRUXTON: That was my clear understanding.

BURR: I thank you for your testimony, sir. If it please the court, I have no wish to question the Commodore further.

Several prosecution witnesses were men from the West to whom Burr had spoken too freely, and they testified flatly that he had planned to establish his own empire, making New Orleans his capital and incorporating large portions of the Louisiana Territory into his realm.

The defense realized it would be impossible to force these men to alter their testimony, so a different technique was employed. Again Burr himself was active in the cross-questioning, and he cleverly attacked the credibility of the witnesses. One man was old and infirm; another was said by his neighbors to lack a sound mind. Even Blennerhassett, whose testimony could have been crippling, was identified by men who had known him for many years as an eccentric who lacked common sense.

Whenever the opportunity arose, the defense launched strong counterattacks. Burr and his counsel repeatedly stressed that the prosecution was failing in its efforts to prove that an overt act of treason had been committed. At one point a full two weeks was devoted to an esoteric legal wrangle, and every authority in the long history of Anglo-Saxon law was cited, studied, and analyzed.

General Wilkinson was reluctant to testify again, undoubtedly because he was afraid that his own participation in the plot would become more clearly defined. But the prosecution did not hesitate to call him to the stand for a second time, and he told substantially the same story he had related to the grand jury. The defense, treating him with open contempt, merely established that President Jefferson had appointed him Governor of the Upper Louisiana Territory, and as in the instance of William Eaton, a distinct impression was left with the jury that Wilkinson had been rewarded by the administration in return for his agreement to damn Aaron Burr.

The usually serene Thomas Jefferson also presented the defense with ammunition that was effective. It was rumored — and Burr's counsel took pains to repeat these stories to the Chief Justice and the jury — that the President promised to pardon a number of men who had taken part in the conspiracy, provided they testified against the defendant. Jefferson refused to dignify these charges by denying them, but he made no secret of his contempt for his former Vice-President, and on a number of occasions it was possible for witnesses for the defense to comment, on the record, to the effect that the President informed visitors he hoped Aaron Burr would be hanged.

On August 27 the prosecution presented a summary of its arguments, and the defense was convinced that Hay had failed to establish his case. The next morning Edmund Randolph counterattacked, pointing out the legal discrepancies and inadequacies found in the position of his opponents. That afternoon Luther Martin presented the final summary. His appeal was emotional and unrestrained, and he concluded in a wild burst of oratory:

> God of Heaven! Have we already arrived at a period when a trial in a court of justice where life is at stake shall be but a solemn mockery, a merely idle form and ceremony to transfer innocence from the jail to the gibbet in order to gratify popular indignation excited by bloodthirsty enemies?
>
> When the sun shines mildly upon us, when the gentle zephyrs play around us, we can easily proceed forward in the straight path to our duties; but when bleak clouds enshroud the sky with darkness, when the tempest rages, when the winds howl and the waves break over us — when the thunders awfully roar over our heads and the lightnings of heaven blaze about us — it is then that the energies of the human soul are called into action. It is then that the truly brave man stands firm at his post. It is then that by the unshaken performance of his duty, man approaches nearest possibility to divinity.
>
> May that God who now looks down upon us, who has in His infinite wisdom placed you in the seat to dispense justice to your fellow citizens… may that God so illuminate your understandings that you may know what is right, and nerve your souls with firmness and fortitude to act according to that knowledge.

Reeking of righteousness and the rum he used to fortify his own soul, Luther Martin resumed his seat.

Chief Justice Marshall adjourned the court until the following day at noon. Then, when the jury reconvened, he read his instructions to them from a long opinion he had just written, a document so exhaustive that its reading lasted for more than three hours. His major points were clear. "To advise or procure a treason is not treason in itself," he declared. He also emphasized that the prosecution had not established as a hard fact the commitment of the overt act of treason. Finally, he directed the jury to find a verdict of guilty or not guilty as their own consciences directed.

Aaron Burr and his counsel exchanged small but elated smiles as the jury filed out of the main chamber of the House of Burgesses. The Chief Justice's directive had been precise, and not even a juryman unversed in the law could mistake his meaning.

Court was adjourned until the jury reported, and Burr retired to a private room with his attorneys. There is no record of what took place behind the closed doors of that room, but the sounds of loud laughter could be heard, and it was assumed that the defense was already celebrating a victory.

The jury returned after an absence of two hours to report a finding of not guilty, and Aaron Burr walked out of the courtroom a free man.

His triumph was highly qualified, however. No man in the United States doubted that he had planned to establish his own nation, which would have included portions of the Louisiana Territory belonging to the United States and parts of Mexico acquired by conquest. Even illiterates knew he had been set free on a technicality, that he had been found not guilty because his scheme had been disrupted before he could put it into operation.

The Republican-Democratic supporters of President Jefferson were wildly indignant. In New York, Philadelphia, Baltimore, and a number of other cities, bonfires were lighted, and Burr, Chief Justice Marshall, and Luther Martin were hanged in effigy. A wave of indignation rolled across the West, too, and in Kentucky, Ohio, and Tennessee men swore they would shoot Aaron Burr on sight if he ever reappeared there.

New England's reaction was more restrained, but even the most ardent Federalists felt a sense of moral revulsion and washed their hands of the former Vice-President. A similar feeling manifested itself throughout the South, which had sympathized with Burr because of the treatment he had received after his duel with Alexander Hamilton. It was unfair for a man to be treated as a pariah because he had killed another in an honorable duel, the South believed, but it was a far different matter for a loyal citizen of the United States — a man who held high public office — to betray his trust and actively plot the dismemberment of his country for his own profit. Feelings were so intense that in Charleston Burr's son-in-law found it politic to issue a statement denying any knowledge of the conspiracy.

The anger, hatred, and loathing that Burr inspired during and after his trial persisted long after his own day. Only in New York City, a pragmatic community that thought only in terms of the present and forgot the past, did the public show indifference to his crimes after the passage of a few years. Elsewhere the anti-Burr sentiments persisted until the eve of the Civil War, when far more important issues caused both North and South to dismiss from memory the Vice-President who had been a traitor to his country.

It was Benedict Arnold rather than Aaron Burr whose name became synonymous with that of traitor. This may have been due to the fact that Arnold's treason was demonstrable, and he actually changed sides during the War of Independence. Another possible reason was that Burr's potential for the achievement of true, lasting immortality was so great that even those who despised him felt strong twinges of sympathy for him as they thought of what he might have been.

This simultaneous tug in two directions was best expressed, perhaps, a generation after Aaron Burr's own day when the Reverend Edward Everett Hale, a distinguished Massachusetts clergyman and author, nephew of the greatest of American orators, Edward Everett, wrote a short story that created an overnight sensation and subsequently became a classic. It was called "The Man without a Country," and Hale freely admitted he had used Aaron Burr as the model for his leading character.

Certainly no man could have been more surprised than Burr himself by the public reaction to his acquittal. He rejoiced because he was free, of course, and accompanying Luther Martin to Baltimore, he indicated in a letter to Theodosia that he was considering a number of plans for the future. Any one of these, he declared, would rehabilitate his name, retrieve his honor, and earn him a fortune.

The persisting tenor of the feelings that surged up against him whenever he appeared in public or his name was mentioned caused him to reevaluate those plans. Ladies snubbed him, honorable men either turned aside or spat at his feet, and even small children jeered at him. On one occasion he saw himself hanged in effigy in a Baltimore square and was thankful he had not been recognized by the crowd, which would have become ugly had his identity become known.

He had overcome other crises, including the killing of Alexander Hamilton, and his minor escapades had been forgiven. But his fellow citizens were determined to punish him for his treasonable transgressions, and he found himself outside the pale, shunned in business, political, and intellectual circles and regarded as a social pariah.

Chapter 18

The United States government and the governments of several states were not yet finished with Aaron Burr. He was indicted for treason and conspiracy in Kentucky and Ohio, and the legislature of Tennessee promised to charge him, too, when it reconvened after a recess. President Jefferson sent a special message to the Congress, urging that a joint committee of the Senate and House be formed to pursue the entire matter by conducting an exhaustive investigation, and the committee was set up without delay.

Burr was irritated by the moves of his enemies, but if he was alarmed, he did not show it. Under Anglo-Saxon common law, he stated, a man could not be tried twice for the same offense, but his foes were so determined to destroy him that they set themselves above the law.

If the people could not snare him by fair means, they were prepared to use foul, and so many threats were made against Burr's life in Baltimore that Martin and the clerks in his office feared for his safety. In spite of his bitter protests, they smuggled him out of town, placing him, in disguise, on a commercial coach bound for Philadelphia. They were just in time. As the coach departed, Burr was treated to the unnerving sight of a lynching party marching down the street in the direction of Martin's office.

That mob finally conveyed the gravity of his situation to him. Therefore he took no chances after his arrival in Philadelphia, where he had previously been honored as a senator and as Vice-President of the United States. He literally sneaked into town, then rented a shabby garret room for himself under an assumed name and made no attempt to get in touch with any of his old friends.

His situation, aside from the dangers, was still desperate. He was virtually penniless, having borrowed two hundred dollars from Martin before leaving Baltimore, and he had no more money to his name. His debts were enormous, bailiffs in several states were hunting for him, and incarceration in a debtors' prison loomed as a probability as soon as his whereabouts became known. His helplessness was increased by the knowledge that for the present he had no way to earn or otherwise obtain funds. It was absurd to think of returning to his private law practice, he had no money to invest in merchant shipping or other commercial enterprises, and he knew no professions other than the law.

He spent his days in his garret room, reading, sometimes writing letters, and always brooding. Afraid that he might be recognized on the streets, he ventured out only after dark and ate his one meal a day in rough, inexpensive taverns which catered to sailors and day laborers. He had been sinking for a long time, and now, at long last, he had struck bottom.

A very few old friends remained loyal to him, or at least felt sorry for him. One of them was Charles Biddle, who, in a manner unknown to posterity, traced him to his Philadelphia rooming house. Biddle scarcely recognized the dejected, hollow-cheeked man who greeted him at the door of the garret room. The shattering of Burr's dreams had destroyed his ebullience, and he was so dispirited that Biddle was afraid he might try to do away with himself.

Attempts to persuade him to part with his dueling pistols failed, however; Burr insisted his weapons were his "only true friends," and he hinted he might have use for them in the very near future. His pride would not permit him to accept help from Biddle, but the Philadelphia aristocrat told other old friends about his plight, and soon a steady stream of callers appeared at the rooming house. Some brought him new clothes; others carried hampers filled with meat, bread, and bottles of wine; and a few discreetly tucked small purses into corners of the hampers.

The news that Burr was living in a Philadelphia garret spread quickly, although nothing about him appeared in print, and the bailiffs were among the first to learn where to find him. He was served with a number of subpoenas in the early autumn of 1807, and it appeared inevitable that he would be sentenced to debtors' prison. But a group of old friends who carefully concealed their identities from him — and from the pubic — posted bonds for him, so he remained technically free, at least for the moment.

At this unhappy juncture, while he was wallowing in the worst misery he had ever known, Aaron Burr opened his garret door one day to find a new visitor on the threshold — Harman Blennerhassett, whose ruin was as great as his own. Whether Burr recognized his responsibility for the plight of the genial eccentric is unknown, but there was no one he less wanted to see, even though Blennerhassett, knowing that misery loved company, had come to him for no reason other than mutual commiseration.

Blennerhassett's reception is best described in his own words, which he recorded in his journal, a diary he never expected other eyes to see:

> ... I am again disposed to call Burr at times deranged, as the only means of accounting for his occasional rashness. Certain I am that he exhibits every derangement except that of avoidable hazard. His energies are little except in his reveries. Out of them he tells different stories to different persons,

enjoining confidence from all, but committing himself in nothing to anyone. Burr is as careless of his facts as of his religion, where neither is exposed to scrutiny. Is he really deranged, I wonder, or does he pretend so that he may escape one who reminds him of the catastrophes in his recent past? I am certain only that this arch-fiend is capable of any deception if it serves his purpose!

Blennerhassett, of all men, was biased against Burr, but his ruminations were honest. He, like all other outsiders, had no idea what might be taking place in the mind of the "arch-fiend."

This disciple of Satan, as he was called in many newspaper accounts, soon learned that Philadelphia was no more disposed to give him sanctuary than Baltimore had been. When his whereabouts became known, he finally dared to venture abroad in daylight, but the reactions of Philadelphians were discouraging. Ladies and gentlemen, many of whom had entertained him when he had been senator and then Vice-President, preferred to cross the street rather than exchange greetings with him. A band of merchant seamen appeared at his rooming house late one night, intending to tar and feather him, but were driven off by the constabulary, who had been maintaining a watch on the place around the clock, having suspected that trouble might develop. The city fathers of Philadelphia had no desire to accept responsibility for the health of the notorious Colonel Burr, and a representative of the mayor called on him to inform him that his presence was not welcome in the City of Brotherly Love.

Given no choice, Burr was forced to move again, and his options were dwindling. Again donning a disguise, he made his way to New York for the first time since the death of Alexander Hamilton and found a temporary hiding place in the home of his faithful crony, Samuel Swartwout. There he spent his days behind closed shutters, receiving calls from a small band of faithful subordinates from the days of his glory.

Stripped of all illusions, unable to conjure up new dreams, Burr was forced to face a set of alarming realities. He was still under indictment in New York and New Jersey on charges of murder in the first degree. A congressional investigation of his conspiracy was under way, and the Republican-Democrats were showing remarkable agility and vigor in their attempts to find evidence that would send him to the gallows. He was wanted for treason in Ohio, Kentucky, Tennessee, and the Louisiana Territory. Suits against him for civil debts were on file in Connecticut, New York, New Jersey, Pennsylvania, Virginia, Maryland, and South Carolina. He had no cash in hand other than small sums he had borrowed and was continuing to borrow, and he could see no way out of his financial dilemma. His name was anathema to respectable men everywhere, and honorable citizens, regardless of their political affiliations, would have no intercourse with him. Ladies were no longer charmed by him, and his enemies were so determined not to let his crimes be forgotten that the newspapers in a score of the nation's largest cities found excuses to damn him daily.

Many months earlier, prior to his last, catastrophic trip to the West Burr had frequently spoken in terms of traveling to Europe for the purpose of seeking the support of foreign governments for his wild venture. Now, in the autumn of 1807, he again contemplated the prospects of travel abroad, this time because life in the United States had become untenable.

His departure was delayed, however, by the sudden illness of his beloved daughter. Her father's tribulations had caused what would be called a nervous breakdown in a later age, and Burr's anxiety about her health was so great he almost lost his own reason. He wanted to go to Charleston, but Alston made it plain to him that the people of South Carolina were very hostile and would give him a rough reception.

So he stayed on at Swartwout's home, sending long, daily letters to his daughter and her husband. By the early spring of 1808 Theodosia had recovered sufficiently to travel, and at her father's repeated insistence she came to New York for a final visit with him before he went off to Europe. She brought her son, now five years old, on the journey with her, and Aaron Burr Alston had a reunion with his doting grandfather.

Wanting to be alone with these two people who meant more to him than all others in the world, Burr resorted to a new ruse and took lodgings in a rooming house near Wall Street under the name of G. H. Edwards. Theodosia posed as his sister, moving into the suite with him under the name of Miss Mary Ann Edwards. However, Burr was as careless in this minor deception as he had been in his conspiracy, forgetting people would think it strange that Miss Edwards had a son of five who bore a strong resemblance to her supposed brother.

The proprietors of the rooming house failed to learn the true identity of their new lodgers but were certain they were other than they seemed, and made life so unpleasant for them that Burr was forced to move to another place nearby with his daughter and grandson. He was convinced, as was Theodosia, that his enemies were responsible and that they were finding subtle ways to harass him.

For the most part, however, the month he spent with Theodosia and little Aaron restored his spirits and his vigor. In his daughter he found his most adoring, uncritical audience, and his bruised vanity quickly healed. Indictments and investigations no longer oppressed him, and his future was no longer bleak. His imagination emerged unimpaired and unscarred from the battering it had received, and once again it soared.

The two most powerful men on earth, Burr declared, were the Emperor Napoleon, of France, who was the master of Europe, and King George III, of Great Britain, whose realm encompassed more than one fourth of the entire civilized world. In spite of their power and wealth, however, both of these men faced identical problems: It was extraordinarily difficult for them to find competent lieutenants, men of initiative and daring, who were capable of carrying out their wishes and, in times of emergency, acting independently on their behalf.

Now that problem would be solved for one or the other. Aaron Burr, the most brilliant man in the New World, intended to offer his services to both and would enter the employ of the higher bidder. His own country feared his pistol and sword but failed to appreciate his mind and his talents as an administrator. So be it. America's loss would be the gain of either Great Britain or France.

Fortified by his new dreams, Burr bade his. daughter a final farewell on June 7, 1808, taking care to borrow two thousand dollars of his son-in-law's money from her before he set sail for London on a British merchantman. Although neither he nor Theodosia realized it, he was destined never to see her or his grandson again.

It is at this point in Aaron Burr's life that most of the early biographies about him ended their accounts. His political career in the United States had terminated, his power was broken, and he would not influence any future developments in his native land. His life, crowded with drama, came to an end for all practical purposes, according to the nineteenth-century authors. What they failed to realize was that an equally incredible drama would crowd the remaining years of his fantastic life. He was destined to live for another twenty-eight years, adding saga after saga to his stormy story. Few men knew such high adventure, enjoyed such glittering success, or paid such a heavy price for their repeated transgressions.

He lived until the final year of Andrew Jackson's second term as President of the United States and watched the nation emerge from shadows to become the most powerful in the New World. His triumphs in the final decades of his life were few, although scarcely a year passed without its share of adventures; his sufferings would have killed lesser men, and the sorrows he endured would have destroyed anyone who lacked his astonishing resilience.

The long sea voyage to England in the late spring and early summer of 1808 restored Burr's physical vigor after the long months spent hiding in the cramped rooming houses of Philadelphia and New York. Mentally alert now, his mind seething with new ideas to restore his fame and fortune, he engaged quarters for himself in a fashionable district near the Strand and laid his plans for conquering a new world.

He appeared to be in luck. Anthony Merry, formerly the British Minister to the United States, had been transferred to the Foreign Office at home when it had appeared that he might embarrass his government by being called as a witness in the Burr treason trial. Merry could not have been overwhelmed by happiness when his American visitor called on him, but he soon fell under the spell of the familiar Burr charm, and friendly relations were reestablished.

Burr wasted little time before launching into an explanation of his latest scheme. His plan to conquer Mexico had been sound. The administration of the Spanish viceroy there was corrupt, lax, and indifferent to the economic and social plight of the natives, most of them Indians or of Indian descent. The Spanish armies in the New World were lazy, lacked discipline, and had no will for combat.

These observations confirmed all that Merry knew of New Spain in North America, but he was surprised, all the same, by the proposal Burr now advanced.

What would have been effective had he created his own empire would be equally effective on behalf of King George, Burr told him. He would gladly lead an expedition on behalf of Great Britain, conquer Mexico, and add it to the British Empire. He did not hesitate to point out that the United States, growing in wealth and power, would be sandwiched between British Mexico and British Canada and caught in this pincer, could be rendered impotent.

Merry not only agreed with the American's logic but familiar as he was with conditions in the New World, could envision all the possibilities of the plan. He agreed with the scheme in principle, although he admitted that since he was no military expert, the details of the campaign Burr planned to fight were beyond his competence. Unfortunately for the dreamer, Merry had no power and little influence in the councils of the mighty in Great Britain.

He was well acquainted with the men at the top, however, and did not hesitate to introduce the newcomer to them. A private appointment was made for the visitor with George Canning, the intellectual and witty Foreign Secretary, whose character, at least on the surface, was remarkably similar to Burr's. Canning listened to the American's recital, asked occasional, penetrating questions, and jotted down a few notes with a quill pen. He was amiable, although a trifle remote, and

Burr gleaned the impression that he had won a power convert to his cause.

The meeting with Canning opened other doors, and with Merry still helping, Burr next obtained an appointment with the Irish-born Robert Stewart, Viscount Castlereagh, Secretary for War. A handsome, dignified man long overshadowed by the more mercurial Canning until he himself became Foreign Secretary in 1812, the aristocratic Castlereagh at first seemed indifferent to the American's proposals and repeatedly stifled yawns. When his somewhat crestfallen visitor came to the end of his speech, however, the Secretary for War peppered him with quick questions, each of which drilled to the heart of Burr's grand design.

By now the American had taken the measure of his man, and his replies were crisp and succinct. Wasting no words, he demonstrated to the Secretary's complete satisfaction that he had planned with infinite care, forgetting no vital details of a military operation. He knew how many infantrymen he needed, how many cavalrymen, how many sappers and artillerymen. He had calculated the precise quantities of provisions, uniforms, cannon, and munitions that would be required, knew how much space they would fill in the holds of ships, and was able to tell the tonnage of the shipping the expedition would need.

It became obvious that Castlereagh was impressed. He ended the conversation with the remark, "It's a pity you didn't fight on the other side in the late unpleasantness with us, Colonel Burr." Burr came away from that encounter with the impression that he had scored heavily.

Not all of Burr's meetings were formal, and he carried on his campaign while making London's social rounds, too. He met the Home Secretary, Lord Liverpool, at several dinner parties and receptions and lost no opportunity to maneuver the distinguished earl into a corner for a discussion of the benefits Britain would enjoy if she subsidized an invasion of Mexico. He also became acquainted with Lord Hawkesbury, Liverpool's son, then a junior member of the Cabinet, and was even more persuasive in his dealings with the younger man.

Burr's attempts to find an occupation took up only a small part of his time, however. He spent most of his days and evenings in pleasure-seeking, somewhat surprised to learn that he was accepted without question in the highest social circles. He succeeded in charming such prominent hostesses as Lady Holland and soon received more invitations to teas, dinners, and galas than it was possible for him to accept.

Early in his London sojourn he also found time to pay a call on the philosopher he had long admired, William Godwin, and they quickly became friends. Many years later Godwin's daughter, Mary, who would marry the great Romantic poet Percy Bysshe Shelley and would herself become the author of *Frankenstein*, recalled that Colonel Burr was a frequent visitor to the house of her father and stepmother. She also remembered that his manners were exquisite and that he had a special talent for storytelling that caused all young children to flock to him.

Burr's letters to Theodosia were filled with self-confidence, and for once his optimism did not appear to be unwarranted. Powerful Cabinet officers were treating his suggestions seriously, while lords and ladies of impeccable social standing opened their doors to the man who had become a pariah in the United States. Godwin and the members of his literary circle — among them Samuel Taylor Coleridge and Charles Lamb — regarded him as a fellow intellectual. In Britain, he told his daughter in a letter overflowing with euphoria, he had at last found his true spiritual home, the one place he had ever known where his soul was at peace. Now, if only she and his grandson could join him, life would be perfect.

What he did not yet know was that his blissful existence was only skin deep. Apparently it did not occur to him that the highest British authorities were aware of all he had done and all that had happened to him in the United States or that they considered him unreliable, shifty, and dangerous.

Chapter 19

One morning late in 1808, while Aaron Burr was enjoying a hearty English breakfast in his lodgings off the Strand, two soberly dressed gentlemen from Lord Liverpool's Home Office paid an unexpected call on him. They showed him their credentials, then produced a long form and began asking him a series of questions. At first Burr replied willingly, thinking that a normal procedure was being followed, but when the questioning became sharper, he asked the reason for the interrogation.

He was informed that the Home Office was taking the legal steps necessary to deport him from the British Isles as an undesirable alien.

As soon as he recovered from his initial shock, Burr sounded the call to battle against the Home Office. He was as familiar with the intricacies of Anglo-Saxon common law as any lawyer in England, and he actually relished the opportunity to match wits with the Home Office and the Attorney General.

Counterattacking without delay, he filed a petition with the Home Office, denying the right of His Majesty's government to deport him. He had been "born within the King's allegiance," he declared. Therefore he "claimed the privileges of a British subject as a birthright."

He had resorted to legal sleight of hand of the first order, and his petition raised questions of principle that threw the entire Cabinet into an uproar. Lawyers on the staff of the Home Office found themselves unable to solve the problem, and other government departments were asked to contribute their opinions. Knowing precisely what he was doing, Aaron

Burr had pinched one of the most sensitive legal-political nerves in Great Britain.

Was an American citizen born prior to the War of Independence still a British subject if he chose to exercise the prerogative of choice? Was he still a British subject, at least in British eyes, regardless of whether he elected to claim Crown protection? These questions reopened the wounds inflicted by the defection of the American Colonies and the establishment of the young nation in the New World, a subject most Englishmen in high places would have preferred to forget.

Now that the Pandora's box had been opened, however, it could not be ignored. A long, complicated debate ensued in Whitehall, and the various government ministries found it almost impossible to reach an agreement in their interpretation of the problem. The lawyers on the staff of the Home Office believed that a rebel who recanted had the right to resume the mantle of a British subject. The Attorney General and his assistants demurred, stating that the privilege was canceled when a rebel took an oath of allegiance to another government. The office of the Lord Chancellor found merit in both positions and could not decide between them.

Lord Hawkesbury, who would become England's leading statesman after he succeeded to his father's title, impatiently brushed aside the entire controversy. Burr's claim, he said, was "picayune, absurd, and monstrous" and should be "disallowed forthwith." He reminded his colleagues that Colonel Burr had held the second highest office in the United States, which reduced his claim to "brazen chicanery," and he urged that the subject be treated with "the contempt he deserves."

The dispute became common knowledge in high social circles and actually increased Burr's popularity. Few individuals could create such a ferment in the government, and ladies and gentlemen who were weary of the interminable war with Napoleon were diverted by the spectacle of the American David pitting his skill against the might of the British Goliath.

"Were there more hours in the day," Burr said in a letter to Theodosia, "I would busy myself from dawn to dawn at the homes of a score or more of the gentry, who beg me to dine and sup with them." He did not exaggerate, but the making of incessant social rounds soon palled on him.

It was at this time that Burr became the friend of the man whose intellect he admired more than that of any other Englishman. He had read everything ever published by the utilitarian philosopher Jeremy Bentham, England's most devastating critic of legal, political, and economic institutions, including those writings too inflammatory to be published in England, which had been printed in France. Bentham, now sixty years old, had achieved an enormous reputation abroad but had not yet won the recognition due him in England and was flattered by the praise heaped on him by the former Vice-President of the United States.

It has been said that Aaron Burr deliberately played on Bentham's vanity for his own ulterior purposes, but a close study of the situation does not substantiate this assertion. The attempt of the Home Office to expel him as an undesirable alien and his counterclaim of British citizenship in no way militated against the prospects for the realization of his Mexican expedition — at least in his own opinion. His letters to Theodosia at this time confidently predicted that the legal question would be decided in his favor and that once this trifling obstacle was removed, he would win official sanction of his Mexican venture.

For more than a quarter of a century Burr's correspondence had expressed his high regard for Bentham, whom he frequently quoted, and his undiminished enthusiasm for the work of the philosopher until the end of his own life strongly indicates that his admiration was sincere and wholehearted. It should be kept in mind, too, that Bentham was a shrewd judge of people, and it is a disservice to him to suggest he might have been fooled by false flattery.

Burr was ecstatic because he could discuss matters of the mind with a great master, and Bentham was pleased because he had found an intellectual equal. Genius met genius, sparks were struck, and the two men forged a close bond which was personal as well as intellectual.

Bentham became so fond of the American, in fact, that when he learned of Burr's precarious financial state, he invited him to share his own home, a modest house on a quiet London residential square. Burr felt honored and accepted the invitation, quickly dropping away from his acquaintances in high society.

The friendship flourished, and Bentham not only provided his guest with shelter and board, but frequently lent him money and even extended an invitation to Theodosia, her husband, and their son to visit him. Only the uncertain state of merchant shipping caused by the violence of the sea warfare being waged by Britain and France prevented the visit from materializing.

As the American and his host drew closer together, Burr confided his schemes to Bentham. At first the philosopher was inclined to believe that his guest was indulging in a literary dream of utopia but gradually came to realize he was in earnest. Years later, after long rumination on the matter, Bentham said, "He really meant to make himself Emperor of Mexico. He told me I should be his principal legislator, and that he would send a ship-of-war to fetch me and bring me to Mexico."

Perhaps the most astonishing of Aaron Burr's personality traits was his continuing, compulsive ability to delude himself. He had lost his reputation, his place in American politics, and his fortune because of his inability to distinguish reality from the make-believe world of his imagination, but he had learned literally nothing from his bitter, disillusioning experiences.

Common sense should have told him that Great Britain had no intention of providing support for a venture conducted by a man who was on the verge of being deported from England as an undesirable alien. Furthermore, he had received no real encouragement for his scheme in high official circles. Cabinet members had treated him with polite kindness, but the most that could be said was that they had congratulated him on the thoroughness of his planning. He had not heard one word or received a single communication even hinting that London might offer him support of any kind. Yet, in his own mind he was certain approval would be forthcoming momentarily, and he would soon begin active preparations for a campaign destined to make history. As Bentham shrewdly observed, he was blind to everything he had no desire to see.

Not even the most determined of dreamers could bury his head in the sands of his own creation permanently, however, and by December, 1808, Burr was forced to concede to Bentham and then to himself that His Majesty's government intended to give him no help. The time had come to make a new assessment of his situation.

He had borrowed more than he could reasonably ask from Jeremy Bentham, and he finally awakened to the realization that he had acquired a number of creditors in London, who, like their counterparts in the United States, were demanding payment for his new clothes, the extravagant gifts he had sent to his daughter and grandson, and the expensive meals he had eaten in some of the city's finest taverns and inns. English debtors' prisons had no more appeal to him than those in his own country, so he formulated the idea of visiting other parts of the British Isles.

He procrastinated until bailiffs visited Bentham's house, searching for him, and then he fled. Long practice had made him expert in the fine art of avoiding creditors, and he resorted to one of his old tricks, moving from one lodging to another and changing his name each time he moved. The sport offered him no satisfaction, however, so he thought seriously about going on a sight-seeing tour of the provinces and Scotland.

The principal drawback to this plan was a lack of funds. But poverty did not deter the resourceful Aaron Burr, and the method used to finance his journey was the most audacious he had yet devised. His dispute with the Home Office had made it necessary for him to report regularly to a small bureau of that department known as the Alien Office, whose director was a civil servant named John Reeves. Burr had made it his business to exert his charm on Reeves, who had actually become his friend. Now, faced with the need for cash, the American outdid himself and applied to Reeves for a substantial loan. The most astonishing aspect of the story is that Reeves complied with the request.

Burr began to keep an ironic diary on this journey, calling it his journal, and he wrote in it regularly for all the years of his long sojourn in Europe, including the detailed accounts of his love affairs and liaisons with many women. As nearly as can be ascertained, he wrote the journal principally for his own amusement, although he sent copies of expurgated portions to Theodosia and his grandson for their entertainment and enlightenment. Few documents ever penned have so completely expressed an author's vanity or his contempt for the rest of mankind; only on rare occasions did Burr fail to pat himself on the back, and even more infrequently did he say a kind word about someone else. It becomes easier to see him in proper perspective when it is realized that he regarded most of his fellow humans as his intellectual and social inferiors — people so stupid and devoid of sensitivity that they could be cheated or fooled at his pleasure.

His first major stop was Oxford, where he spent several happy days in the great libraries of the university; if he had no use for his contemporaries, his reverence for books compensated for his scorn. One evening he dined with a group of divinity students, regaling them with a long speech on freethinking; by the next day he was honest with himself and called his address silly. He went on to Stratford on Avon, where he enjoyed such a hearty dinner that he went to his room and fell asleep, thereby losing the opportunity to go sight-seeing.

Burr's peregrinations took him to Birmingham, which he described as dreary. From that point he traveled leisurely northward, sometimes stopping at inns, at other times using letters of introduction from Jeremy Bentham, John Reeves, and other friends to stay in private homes. At no time did he hesitate to avail himself of the hospitality of those who offered it.

Edinburgh greeted him as a visiting dignitary of the first rank. He was accepted without question in the city's leading social and artistic circles. Dinners and other functions were held in his honor, and prominent hostesses competed with each other for the pleasure of his company.

In the month he spent in Edinburgh he established a friendship with the man who wielded a greater influence than anyone else in the literary world of Great Britain — Francis

Jeffrey, editor of the renowned Edinburgh *Review*, who could make or break the reputation of an author. The cynical, astute Jeffrey found in Aaron Burr an intellect similar to his own, and they spent long evenings together discussing fiction, the drama, poetry, and essays. A few months later Jeffrey declared he had never encountered anyone whose knowledge of literature, classical or modern, was as encyclopedic.

The visitor made a far less favorable impression on Sir Walter Scott, who was already regarded throughout the English-speaking nations as the great novelist of the age. In a letter Scott said:

> Mr. Burr is an arrogant little man totally lacking in humility. He has opinions on all things, does not hesitate to speak his mind, and will not listen to the expression of contrary views. Were it not for his efforts to make himself companionable his company would be insufferable. I do not enjoy him, but I am in a minority here, and meet him whenever I venture abroad. He enjoys the favor of most.

Burr appeared to have given himself up to hedonistic pleasures, and neither his precarious finances nor his future occupation seemed to worry him. Theodosia was concerned about him, however, and in her letters repeatedly urged him to busy himself with gainful activities worthy of his talents. With great delicacy she reminded him that he was fast approaching his fifty-third birthday, and she was saddened because he was creating no solid vocational foundation.

Her father paid no attention to her good advice, perhaps because he felt powerless to overcome new habits and appetites unlike any he had ever before experienced. Throughout his entire life he had needed little sleep, had eaten no more than was necessary, and had been indifferent to whiskey and other liquors, even though he had been a host who had set an elegant and sumptuous table. Now a lifetime of discipline and self-abnegation had come to an end. The tensions of his many years of hard work and attempting to make his wild dreams come true were taking an unexpected toll.

Previously he had needed no more than four hours of sleep a night, but now he required a minimum of seven or eight hours and could not rouse himself in the mornings. He hired people to awaken him and wrote in his journal that one morning in Edinburgh he was called twenty times but was so overcome by lethargy that it was impossible for him to leave his bed. Next he hired a barber to shave him at 6:00 A.M. each day, arranging for the early appointment in an attempt to force himself to leave his bed.

Food and drink assumed a new importance, too. He was ravenously hungry all day. He consumed a hearty breakfast, then was compelled to eat a second because he could not wait until early afternoon for his midday repast. At high tea time he ate everything in sight and was ashamed to admit, even to himself, that his evening dinner was his largest meal of the day. He had not touched sweets since he had been a small boy but now wolfed down rich desserts, almost always taking second and third helpings. Previously contenting himself with a glass or two of watered wine, he drank considerable quantities of claret, port, and brandy and always wanted more.

Burr's journal clearly indicates that he loathed his over-indulgence, but he seemed unable to curb it. Again and again he confessed that he had consumed too much liquor, eaten himself into a somnolent state, and smoked so many *segaros* made of a heavy, black tobacco that he loathed the smell of his own breath.

He had always looked far younger than his years, but now, as he gained weight and became plump for the first time, he appeared to age overnight. He had resembled a man in his thirties when he first sailed to England, but by the time he ended his month's stay in Scotland he looked like one who would never see sixty again. At long last it struck him that he was no longer young, with the better part of his life still in the future, and the realization compounded his unhappiness.

Chapter 20

Burr returned to London after his tour of England and Scotland, assuming that he would take up residence in Jeremy Bentham's house. But the philosopher, although still on friendly terms with him, had no desire to be burdened with someone he privately regarded as slightly mad and politely but firmly made it plain that it would not be convenient to entertain a guest for a protracted period.

Forced to look elsewhere and ever conscious of the fact that bailiffs were searching for him because of his unpaid bills, he called himself Mr. Kirby and took lodgings in the modest home of a lower-class Cockney family, who sold vegetables in the open markets near Drury Lane. Never before had he sunk so low on the social scale, but he convinced himself that at least he had outwitted the bill collectors.

During the long winter of 1808-1809 it gradually dawned on him that he had worn out his social welcome in London. He received few dinner invitations, and when he called on people who had shown him friendship, they greeted him with subtle reserve. He was compelled to rely more and more on himself and turn back to his first love — books. Burying himself in reading, he spent the equivalent of more than one thousand dollars at the shop of a single bookseller and made smaller purchases in other shops.

As usual, he had no cash available and opened accounts at these bookstores. When he failed to pay his bills, his unhappy creditors reported his defections to the authorities. The description of Mr. Kirby closely fitted that of Aaron Burr, for whom the bailiffs were hunting, and Burr somehow learned they were on his trail. The time had come for him to change names and again disappear.

On the evening of April 4, 1809, he was secretly packing his books and clothes when four bailiffs came to the house. Two guarded the entrances so he could not slip away, and the other two hurried to his rooms and placed him under arrest. His precious books, clothes, and personal mementos — including a Vanderlyn portrait of Theodosia — were confiscated, and the former Vice-President of the United States was unceremoniously hauled off to debtors' prison.

Protesting vehemently, he claimed protection as a subject of the King, but the bailiffs and the prison warden ignored his legalistic harangue. Burr found himself confined in filthy quarters with assorted rogues and confidence men and others who had gone bankrupt. His situation, like that of his fellow prisoners, appeared hopeless: Because of his confinement, no inmate of a debtors' prison could earn the money that would pay off his creditors and win his release.

For a miserable forty-eight hours Burr languished in the prison, which was infested with vermin and rats. Convinced he would remain there until he died, he sank into a near stupor and broke down and shed tears.

After another twelve hours of incarceration, however, he was released without advance notice, and his possessions were restored to him. His ego reviving, he immediately assumed he had been set free because of his importance, but he quickly learned otherwise. The Home Office had grown weary of his antics, and he was served with a notice to the effect that His Majesty's government found his presence in England embarrassing. Therefore, the order stated, he would be deported at the expense of the government to Helgoland, a bleak island about fifty-five miles off the coast of Denmark, which was under British occupation.

A future in Helgoland was as empty and unpleasant a prospect as life in prison, and Burr searched desperately for another refuge. He knew he would not be welcome at home, so he made no attempt to return to the United States. It was impossible for him to travel to France or to most other nations on the Continent, which were under French domination. Napoleon had just made his elder brother, Joseph, the King of Spain, and this puppet monarch was already so unpopular that the wily Napoleon had no intention of extending a welcome to the man who had plotted to deprive Spain of her North American empire.

The Swedish Minister to Britain finally took pity on the homeless refugee and granted him a visa. The prospect of visiting a nation about which he knew virtually nothing and cared less did not appeal to Burr, but his choice was limited. He could visit Sweden, accept deportation to Helgoland, or return to an English prison. He chose Sweden.

Traveling there on a Swedish merchantman, he landed at Göteborg on May 30. His unerring instinct for self-preservation had prompted him to obtain letters of introduction to prominent persons in Sweden from English acquaintances who were relieved that he was leaving, and he carried a portfolio bulging with such communications. He also made it his business to learn all he could about Swedish history, government, customs, and the arts, and he applied himself so diligently to a study of the Swedish language that he could understand it and make himself understood in it within a month of his arrival there. Rarely had his ability to concentrate stood him in such good stead.

He left England without regret and noted in his journal, "How these French and English, one by water and the other by land, do torment the whole world!"

When he reached Stockholm, he learned that William Hosack and Thomas Robinson — two other Americans of dubious reputation about whom almost nothing was known except that they, too, lived by their wits — had found asylum on the tolerant shores of Sweden. They were happy to welcome a compatriot, and he gratefully accepted their offer of quarters in the small, unpretentious house they were renting for a modest sum. Hosack and Robinson were heavy drinkers, and for a few days Burr kept pace with them, but he found his lack of self-discipline so disturbing that he forced himself to drink less.

Burr's letters of introduction opened many Swedish doors to him, and hospitable ladies and gentlemen extended many dinner invitations which prevented him from starving to death. His funds were so low now that he usually had an empty purse, and his fellow Americans were no better situated. They ate gooseberries and bread for breakfast but could not afford to buy a meal at noon, and Burr depended on his dinner invitations for his nourishment. He ate enough to suffice for twenty-four hours and consequently became a gourmand, consuming enormous quantities of food at the homes of his kind Swedish hosts. In fact, he ate so much at these dinner parties that he actually gained more weight.

Perhaps the most astonishing aspect of this period of Aaron Burr's life was his own reaction to it. His reputation was in shreds, he had been reduced to the status of a genteel beggar, and he had no future prospects of any kind, but he accepted his fate cheerfully, making light of his hardships and refusing to worry. This attitude was reflected in his journal, as well as in his letters to Theodosia. It could be argued that he dissembled for his daughter's sake, not wanting her to be too concerned about him, but he had no reason to conceal the truth from the pages of his journal, in which his candor was as refreshing as it was brutal.

For the present, at least, he had abandoned his craving for power and his lust for excitement and adventure. He was content to drift, to think of nothing more significant than the problem of where to cadge another dinner invitation. Seen in perspective, it may be that he was enjoying a vacation of sorts; it is difficult to find any other explanation for his lack of pride, his indifference to his fate, his willingness to accept a precarious situation with such good humor and grace.

Even the most hospitable of hosts eventually tired of the company of a perennial guest, no matter how great his charm, and by the early autumn of 1809 Burr realized it was time for him to move on. The Swedes were extending dinner invitations with some reluctance, and he was adept at reading the handwriting on the wall.

By this time the situation in France had changed somewhat, Napoleon having tightened his grip on the always volatile people of Spain. As a result, Burr felt bold enough to believe he could seek assistance from Prince Talleyrand, the French Foreign Minister, and from Jerome Bonaparte, Napoleon's younger brother, both of whom had been his guests in palmier days. He wrote to them, and although neither replied directly, their swift response startled and gratified him.

He was not yet granted permission to visit France, although the French legation in Stockholm hinted that he might not have to wait too long for a visa. Meanwhile, he was given visas for travel in Denmark and the German states. A sudden, unexpected financial windfall also eased his situation. He had offered business advice to a Swedish acquaintance, who had followed his suggestions and made so much money from his deal that he gave Burr the modern-day equivalent of six thousand dollars in gold.

He promptly hired a valet, rented a carriage and a fine team of four horses, and set out for Denmark, accompanied by Hosack and Robinson, whose expenses he paid in return for the favor they had rendered him when they had taken him into their house. The party rode through Denmark in style, making overnight stops at the best inns and dining at fine restaurants.

Eventually they reached the town of Altona, situated directly across the border from the great German port city of Hamburg. A large American colony lived there, comprised in the main of shipowners and traders. When Burr appeared in a tavern they frequented, a delegation visited his table for the purpose of informing him that his presence there was not welcome — that patriotic Americans wanted nothing to do with the notorious Colonel Burr.

Burr returned without delay to Altona, although Robinson and Hosack took up residence in Hamburg, and each day he crossed the border into the German city, taking care to avoid fellow Americans. He became well acquainted with several generals and a number of government officials, and he dined at the residence of the French minister, to whom he applied for permission to visit Paris. His application was forwarded to the Foreign Ministry, and he whiled away the time visiting the great men of Hamburg, cultivating authors, musicians, artists, and noblemen. Never one to stint when he had funds, Burr meticulously returned the hospitality of those who entertained him, and he was so profligate that in three weeks he ran through his six-thousand-dollar gift.

The time had come for him to travel again, he decided, so he borrowed a small sum from Hosack and Robinson, discharged his valet, and set out alone for a tour of Germany, traveling by public carriage. He went, in turn, to Hanover, Brunswick, and Frankfort, and everywhere he moved in the best circles, attending the theater, operas, and concerts, often dining at the palaces of the reigning dukes of various German principalities. At Weimar he met the greatest German author of the age — the poet Johann von Goethe.

They discussed philosophy, politics, and literature, and although Burr was impressed by few men, he wrote to Theodosia that he regarded Goethe as "the best mind of our time."

The poet did not return the compliment, later writing:

> Mr. Burr is a sophist, and one cannot determine his real opinions. There is a contrary streak in his nature that sometimes impels him to argue in favor of a position not out of conviction, but merely because of his passion for debate. One wonders what philosophical principles lie behind his easy, ever-present smile, and one is inclined to suspect, perhaps without just cause and certainty without proof, that no convictions are dear to him.

By this time Burr had become expert in living off the bounty of others. He cadged meals, "borrowed" small sums when he found someone willing to make him a small loan, and bought on credit from shop-owners gullible enough not to demand that he pay them in cash. Exhibiting neither shame nor remorse, he wrote to Theodosia that he left a trail of disappointed, outraged creditors in his wake.

The weeks became months, and Burr seemed to be condemned to an endless life of aimlessness, drifting from one foreign place to another, staying at each until he wore out his welcome, then moving on. Suddenly, in December, 1809, news that electrified all of Europe changed his situation.

The Emperor Napoleon let it be known that he was divorcing Empress Josephine and had contracted an alliance with a princess of the royal house of Hapsburg — Maria Louisa. Not only would the upstart monarch become allied to the oldest and most distinguished of the ruling families on the Continent, but France would become the partner of the powerful Austrian Empire.

Within a year or two Napoleon would become the undisputed master of the entire Continent, and he was determined to destroy Great Britain, the most implacable of his foes. His sea forces were still inferior to the British navy, which made it difficult to maintain close communications with the far reaches of the empire, and Napoleon decided to perform colonial surgery. As his initial act, he announced he was granting independence to Mexico.

The Imperial decree reawakened Aaron Burr's dream and revived his hope of establishing his own domain in North America. He sent letters to everyone he knew in Paris, urging that he be given a French visa without delay and declaring that he, more than any other man on earth, was in a position to perform a service greatly desired by the Emperor Napoleon. He dispatched letter after furious letter and was so insistent that the Foreign Ministry, which no longer had reason to deny him admittance, granted him the necessary visa.

Late in January, 1810, the precious visa secure in his otherwise empty wallet, Aaron Burr set out for Paris and was so anxious to reach the city without delay that he rode horseback on icy roads, proudly informing Theodosia that he made better time than the swiftest of Imperial messengers.

228

Other visitors to Paris, then as later, were impressed by the physical beauty, rich cultural fare, and urbane sophistication of the city, but Burr, again blinded by his dream, was scarcely conscious of his surroundings. He borrowed money from Count Volney, a prominent nobleman who had accepted his hospitality in New York, and with that nest egg rented himself a pleasant suite of rooms on the Left Bank, overlooking the Seine.

His mind working with the same precision and speed he had shown many years earlier in battle as an officer of the Continental Army, he made careful plans, then put them into action. It was no accident that when he attended the theater one night in early February, he occupied the box directly opposite the one in which the Emperor was sitting. During the first intermission he bowed deeply and could see Napoleon asking the identity of the bald, plump foreigner who wore his clothes with such an air.

For ten days Burr neglected his journal and worked almost around the clock to prepare a detailed outline of the most ambitious scheme he had ever conceived. As he had always done in the past, he covered every essential detail, leaving nothing to chance.

When dealing with someone of Napoleon's stature, a man with an imagination more than a match for his own, Burr did not stint. Working continuously, again indifferent to food and sleep, he produced a detailed proposal of more than two hundred finely written pages accompanied by more than forty maps he had accumulated during that same period. This was the supreme trial of his life, and he was convinced that if he failed, he would not have another opportunity to create the empire to which he had so long aspired.

In brief, he prepared an outline of the most audacious and far reaching of all his schemes. He would have no need for French troops or ships, he wrote, because he well knew the Emperor could not spare a single soldier or vessel. All he asked was a substantial sum of money and an initial supply of foodstuffs and munitions for the army he would raise — a force that would live off the land. In return he promised to conquer the entire western hemisphere and acting as Napoleon's viceroy, would add all of North, and South America to the French Empire!

Chapter 21

No one knew better than Burr himself that at first glance his proposal would be regarded as absurd; it was too ambitious, too broad in scope. So he filled in details to give the scheme plausibility and depth. He also appealed to French sentiment by emphasizing that the most important of former French colonies in the New World — Canada and the Louisiana Territory — once again would fly the French ensign. Included in the plan, too, was the step-by-step military campaign he intended to wage simultaneously on two continents, and these maneuvers demonstrated that he had the military foresight of a great general.

He omitted only one aspect of primary importance: He said nothing to indicate how he planned to raise his army. His overall conception was ridiculous, of course. It was the product of the mind of a daydreamer who had lost his grip on reality. Presumably he believed he enjoyed such great popularity with the American public that men by the thousands, perhaps tens of thousands, would flock to his banner when he appeared and issued his call to arms.

He submitted the document to Talleyrand, asking that it be called to the attention of the Emperor without delay. Then, his work temporarily completed, he settled back to enjoy the delights of Paris until, as he confidently expected, his scheme would win Imperial approval. But his immediate prospects were dimmed because in Paris as elsewhere, one needed money for pleasure, and his purse was empty. He did not know many people in France, so he received only two or three dinner invitations each week and again faced the grim prospect of starvation.

Contemplating various ways and means of earning a living, he ruled out all activities that could be considered to be beneath the dignity of the future French viceroy for the entire New World. According to a story that may be apocryphal, he attended a dinner party at the home of a wealthy couple whose dining-room furnace smoked, a condition that a succession of masons and chimney sweeps had been unable to cure. When the American said he could eliminate the smoking, his host wagered one hundred francs in gold that he would fail. Burr, who had no more than a few coppers in his pocket, not only accepted the challenge but actually got rid of the smoke permanently by quickly devising an ingenious flue that connected the chimney with that in the kitchen. His host paid the bet, but Burr laughingly demurred when his hostess, in all seriousness, suggested that he could earn large sums by applying his skill to the many smoking chimneys of Paris. He was pleased that money jingled in his pocket for a few days, but the future master of the West could not soil his hands like a common laborer.

There were other, more dignified ways of earning money, and he accepted an offer, complete with initial payment, from a bookseller who wanted him to translate a volume from English into French. He did enough work to obtain about three quarters of the agreed total, then abandoned the project.

Strict French regulations prohibited the practice of law by foreigners, but Burr soon demonstrated that he could be as adept in finding legal loopholes in France as he had been in avoiding the law in the United States and Great Britain. The Industrial Revolution was stirring in France, as it was elsewhere in the West, and new mechanical inventions were being made daily. Two of the many that were called to Burr's attention appealed to him: One was a method of pumping water to city residents at low cost, and the other was a technique for obtaining vinegar as well as sugar from the sap of trees. He went to both inventors, offered to represent their interests in the United States in return for a fee, and, as a favor, said he would act as their attorney in France.

When members of the bar heard of this unorthodox deal, they complained to the Ministry of Justice. Summoned to the Ministry to explain, he made it clear that he was receiving no recompense for helping the inventors, and rather than representing them as their attorney, he was merely advising them as a friend. The Ministry was helpless and could not bring charges against him.

In at least one instance Burr perpetrated the trickery of an accomplished confidence man. Many years earlier he had been the New York lawyer for a Dutch business concern called the Holland Land Company, which was still active in the sale of tracts to prospective immigrants to the United States. He no longer had any connection with the concern, to be sure, but was familiar with their offerings and business procedures.

So, when an English expatriate living in Paris expressed the desire to settle in the United States and buy land there, Burr saw an opportunity to earn some money and informed the man he was the official representative of the Holland Land Company. The Englishman gladly paid him eight hundred dollars in cash, receiving in return a note from Burr stating that he was acting as an intermediary and would "exert his most forceful efforts" to obtain the necessary deeds for the property.

Hurrying off to Amsterdam, Burr actually attempted to obtain the deeds. He offered to split the fee with the company, making it plain that he had been paid four times the price that the Holland Land executives themselves would have charged for the property in question. Appalled by his machinations and his trickery in overcharging the client, the angry directors of the concern summarily rejected the deal.

Since he realized he would be open to charges of fraud if he returned empty-handed to Paris, Burr persuaded an acquaintance to buy the land for two hundred dollars, which was the actual fee. Then, somewhere in the Amsterdam underworld, he found a forger who altered the face of the document to indicate that the cost had been the full eight hundred dollars. Returning to Paris, he gave the Englishman his deed and pocketed a profit of six hundred dollars, minus only his traveling expenses and the small sum he had been required to pay the forger.

It was of paramount importance, he believed, that he maintain appearances, and in the sixteen and a half months he stayed in Paris he fought an unremitting battle to conceal his abject poverty from French officials who conceivably might be consulted by the Emperor in reference to his ambitious scheme. His success is a tribute to his extraordinary ingenuity and skill, but there is no truth in the legend that his sufferings in Paris transformed him into a noble, compassionate man. He skated on very thin ice at times, but he was beyond possible reformation, and his sufferings were slight.

While awaiting a response from the Emperor, he devoted himself almost exclusively to the task of maintaining appearances. In his lexicon this meant living in as much luxury as he could command. Using his wits and demonstrating remarkable dexterity, he enjoyed great success.

Artist John Vanderlyn, an old friend, was living in Paris, as were several other Americans he had known at home, among them a citizen of Connecticut named Edward Griswold, who was close to his sister and brother-in-law. From time to time he obtained small loans from these compatriots to pay his rent, and having moved to modest lodgings in a fashionable neighborhood, he found it relatively easy to maintain a roof over his head.

Utilizing his charm to enlarge his circle of acquaintances and friends, he made it a habit to call on various prosperous Parisians shortly before their midday meal or evening dinner. Only on rare occasions did they fail to ask him to break bread with them. In fact, he had become so adept in cadging invitations that he could boast to Theodosia: "There are twenty-one principal meals to be eaten each week, excluding afternoon tea, one of the few civilized habits of the English, which I have adopted. Of these twenty-one meals, I have as yet never failed to receive invitations to a minimum of fourteen, and you may rest assured I always accept."

Burr kept supplies of coffee, tea, and bread in his own quarters, and when all else failed, he ate breakfast and took afternoon tea at home. The cost of these supplies was "negligible," he wrote, and he never had to spend more than a few sous per week.

He invariably dressed in the height of fashion and soon acquired a reputation as one of the more elegant gentlemen of Paris. His fellow Americans, knowing his past, assumed he was in debt to every tailor in town, but they were mistaken. The brief time Burr had spent in a London debtors' prison had made him cautious, and he had no desire to repeat the experience in Paris, where such prisons were even meaner. He had also heard that the Parisian bailiffs were far more clever and determined than their counterparts in Great Britain and the United States, so he took no chances and always paid cash for his purchases. It was important to him to maintain a lofty image, since he knew Napoleon would lose interest in him, if not in his scheme, should he be imprisoned and be revealed as a bankrupt.

Although he usually had ample funds in his purse, he refused to divulge to anyone his sources of ready cash. Vanderlyn, Griswold, and others speculated in vain, for Burr confided only in the journal, which he kept locked in a bedchamber cupboard. The source of his income has not surprised later generations aware of his mode of existence and his amazing ability to improvise and contrive. The answer is simple: He earned a steady income by playing cards with wealthy Parisians.

Never before had Burr demonstrated the slightest interest in either of the most popular of card games played in the eighteenth and early nineteenth centuries — whist and the French one-and-twenty. When he saw large sums carelessly changing hands during after-dinner play at many homes, he saw no reason why he shouldn't adopt this means to add to his own income. So he read the few books ever published on the two games and spent many evenings watching others play.

He refused to sit at the gaming tables himself — although repeatedly asked to join — until he knew precisely what moves to make in any given situation. Then, because of his amazing intellectual dexterity and the trained and unerring quality of his play, he allowed himself to be drawn into the games. His success from the outset was phenomenal, and he won so often that a few losers suspected he cheated. He knew they were muttering about him, but he wrote to Theodosia that there was no grain of truth in their suspicions; there was no need for him to cheat, since he could win easily by relying on his skill. In other words, he intimated that he would not have hesitated to cheat had it been necessary.

Burr attributed his great success at cards to three rules of his own making, all of which he took care to observe. First, he never boasted and always attributed a winning streak to luck, never allowing other players to guess that his knowledge of the odds in games of chance was far superior to the little they knew. Second, he never played recklessly, no matter how great the temptation to make a quick killing, even when the odds were in his favor; he might gamble wildly in politics but held himself in check when playing whist or one-and-twenty. Finally, he took care never to win too much from one opponent at a single sitting.

His success was all the more remarkable because he possessed no funds as a reserve. He literally had no choice when he played: He *had* to win because he had no cash to pay off his debts if he happened to lose. And he knew that no gentleman would consent to sit at the table with him again if he failed to pay on any losing occasion.

There were times, of course, when he encountered others who had acquired formidable reputations as card players, but he always found seemingly valid reasons not to match wits and skills with such experts. He would either plead indisposition or claim another engagement that forced him to cut the evening short. Had he shown the same caution in handling his career that he demonstrated in his card playing, his life would have been far different.

When his card-playing friends were unavailable or out of the city, Burr found other ways to obtain small sums of money, never quite realizing he was living a hand-to-mouth existence. More than once he pawned his watch, retrieving it after a successful evening at the gaming table. On one occasion, when he was particularly desperate, he sold a number of Swedish, Danish, and German coins he had been collecting for his grandson. Later, writing to Theodosia about the incident in detail, he exhibited no sorrow, bluntly stating that the francs he had received in return had filled his larder, provided him with an excellent dinner, and enabled turn to lay in a small store of wines.

With his infinite capacity for self-delusion Burr managed to convince himself that Napoleon would eventually rule in favor of his enterprise and that only more preying problems prevented the Emperor from acting immediately. His situation was similar to that which he had endured in England: He received no encouragement from the Foreign Ministry or any other government bureau, but his fertile imagination kept his hopes alive.

One serious matter caused him untold suffering. He received no letters from Theodosia, although he felt certain she was writing to him. He worried incessantly, finally persuading himself that a cabal of American and British shipowners who held contracts for the delivery of transatlantic mail had been formed for the purpose of denying him his correspondence. Many months passed before it occurred to him that the highly efficient French secret police, one of the best-organized arms of Napoleon's government, were intercepting his incoming mail, reading it, and then destroying it without allowing him to receive it.

Most Parisians, like the foreigners who lived in the city, took great pains to insure that their paths did not knowingly cross those of the secret police. The Emperor was more concerned about the principles of individual liberty than any French ruler who had preceded him, but in spite of his devotion to freedom of religion and other causes, he dealt mercilessly with anyone suspected of opposition to him. Men of substance — Frenchmen and foreigners alike — had been known to vanish from their homes without a trace and subsequently were found in prison or exile. So the wise walked with a wary tread.

Aaron Burr offered no threat to Napoleon, to be sure, but his past record caused the secret police to suspect that he might turn against the Emperor at any time, and they kept him under tight surveillance. A man who had betrayed his own country after holding the second highest office in the land was one who had the potential for engaging in a conspiracy against the ruler of a nation where he was a guest.

What Burr failed to realize was that his letters to Theodosia met the same fate as her communications addressed to him. For a long time he mailed his letters in the full expectation they would cross the Atlantic, and he had no way of knowing that although he wrote regularly and frequently, his daughter had not been receiving any mail from him.

In time, however, he began to wonder whether Theodosia was receiving mail from him. Though he had no proof that the French were reading and confiscating his letters, he nevertheless took steps to circumvent the secret police, meeting trickery with trickery. He disguised his handwriting, put the names of nonexistent persons on the backs of his envelopes, and even persuaded friends to mail his letters for him. But the secret police were familiar with such stratagems and managed to intercept all of his correspondence.

The efficiency of the secret police caused great hardship for Theodosia. She worried about her father and lived in dread that the worst had happened to him. She read rumors about him in the American newspapers and had no way of determining whether they were true or false. According to some, Napoleon had given him a government post; others said that King George III had granted him a handsome pension; still others insisted he was leaving Europe and intended to sail to Charleston to join her. One persistent account stated that he had gone to Spain and was working with men of high rank there to outfit an expedition that would reclaim Mexico for Spain.

Chapter 22

In February, 1811, the fifty-six-year-old Aaron Burr fell to his lowest state, and his situation became truly desperate. His physical and mental distress was acute, and for the only time in his life he seriously contemplated suicide as the only way to end his suffering.

He had lost all of his teeth, and a set of false dentures made for him by a Paris dentist who had demanded a cash payment in full had emptied his purse. A severe attack of the ague had kept him in bed for almost three weeks, making it impossible for him to accept dinner invitations or put a little money in his pocket at the gaming table. In spite of his weakened physical condition he could no longer enjoy a night's sleep; this was the beginning of an incurable insomnia which plagued him for the rest of his life.

He had been forced to pawn his greatcoat in order to pay his rent, and he lacked the money to retrieve his boots from a shoemakers where they had been taken by a chambermaid for repairs. He was so poor he could afford little firewood, and his room was so cold he was forced to spend most of his waking hours in bed. For sustenance he lived on bread, coffee, and tea.

His physical condition had deteriorated, too. What was left of his hair had turned white, and he suffered from attacks of indigestion that gave him no peace, regardless of whether he ate a full meal or had to content himself with a chunk of bread and bitter coffee. He walked with a limp, the permanent effect of an injury to his ankle suffered while trying to board a public coach in too much of a hurry.

A brief line in his journal, written in late February, 1812, and soon thereafter repeated in a letter to his daughter, indicates the depths to which he had sunk: "I have worked and wept and torn the paper and thrown myself down in despair, and rose up full of some new thought, and tried again and failed again, till my heart is worn out with constant renewal of the same scene."

It was at this critical time in his life that his dream of attaining power and glory finally died. His desperate situation forced him to face reality at last, and he realized that Napoleon had no intention of employing him in the New World or anywhere else. He could not return to Great Britain, and no other nation wanted anything to do with him. Sleepless and hungry, half-frozen and in constant pain, he permanently abandoned all hope of making himself emperor of his own realm.

A careful assessment of his dilemma, its urgency sharpening his wits, caused Burr to realize there was just one place he wanted to go: home. His roots were in the United States, his daughter and grandson were there, and he was tired of living a tacky, precarious existence abroad.

He needed money to pay his bills in Paris and to purchase his passage, to be sure, and he also needed two vital documents. One was a visa that would enable him to leave France, and he knew it would not be granted if he still owed a sou to anyone in the country. The other was a passport to readmit him to the land of his birth.

Reduced to the final degradation, he was forced to borrow money from the chambermaid in order to retrieve his boots. Then, shivering in the cold without his greatcoat, he went on foot to the Ministry of the interior and to the United States Legation to make his application for the necessary papers. He also began to scout around for some means of obtaining a loan.

Several French ministries breathed more easily when they learned that the American trouble maker wanted to leave France, and the loan became the least of Burr's concerns. To his surprise, one of the first acquaintances to whom he applied, the Duc de Bassano, advanced him the large sum of ten thousand francs in gold. Burr did not know it, but the French government quietly reimbursed Bassano.

Bureaucratic red tape and inefficiency caused endless delays. The Ministry of the Interior replied with unexpected speed and granted the exit visa in March but six weeks later canceled it because the original application had been lost in the files, and Colonel Burr was asked to submit another application. Late in March an official of the United States Legation, Jonathan Russell, issued a passport, and a vastly relieved Aaron Burr bought passage on a ship sailing from Amsterdam. Subsequent delays in procuring the exit visa forced him to transfer his passage to another ship scheduled to sail at a later date.

In June he was summoned to the legation, and Russell informed him that because of the mounting ill-feeling between the United States and Great Britain, American citizens were being permitted to leave Europe only on merchant ships that were least likely to be met and taken into custody by the British navy. Consequently no Americans were being allowed to sail from such northern ports as Amsterdam, and Colonel Burr's passport was amended, making it mandatory that he sail from Bordeaux.

The tragicomedy of errors continued. The owners of the vessel on which he had booked passage refused to return Burr's money, which made it imperative that he sail from Amsterdam rather than Bordeaux. Russell, who held a low opinion of Colonel Burr, refused to listen to his pleas or change his passport. Realizing that this might be his last chance to return home, Burr became panicky.

In a ploy worthy of a French farce, he learned the name of a beautiful French lady with whom Russell was in love and secretly appealed to her for assistance. She took pity on him, and although he did not learn what she said to Russell, the change was made in his passport within a few days.

He left France in July and hurried to Amsterdam. There he learned that the ship's captain had been sent to a debtors' prison, making it impossible for the ship to sail until a new master was found. Burr's funds were virtually depleted again, so he pawned his watch and sold the remaining coins he had hoarded for his grandson. He obtained enough money to win the release of the ship's captain from jail and felt infinite relief as he finally stepped onto the deck of the merchantmen.

However, his troubles were just beginning. A few hours after the brig weighed anchor, she was taken into custody by a warship of the British navy as she emerged from the Zuider Zee. A prize crew was sent aboard, and the captured merchantman was brought to the English port of Yarmouth as a prize.

England was the last place on earth Aaron Burr wanted to go, but he had no voice in the matter, and he was afraid that he would be taken into custody and sent to debtors' prison as soon as his identity became known. Even worse, the British government might apprehend him and hold him indefinitely as an undesirable alien. So he gave a false name when he landed, pretending he was a New Englander named Adolphus Arnot. The immigration authorities released him, ordering him to report to the Alien Office in London.

Badly frightened, Burr hastened to London from Yarmouth, and when he arrived in the city, he had only two shillings in his pocket. His situation was worse than he had imagined possible, and the nightmare appeared to be endless. He went straight to Jeremy Bentham, who took him in, fed him a hearty meal, and agreed to shelter him until he could make other arrangements. John Reeves, of the Alien Office, also felt sorry for him and wrote in his record book that one Adolphus Arnot had arrived in England through no will of his own. Other friends rallied to Burr's cause, too, and gave him enough money to move out of Bentham's house and rent lodgings of his own.

Once again he was forced to follow the old, sad routine of cadging meals where he could, meanwhile keeping a supply of bread and coffee in his room so he would not starve on those days when no one invited him to dine.

His rounds were severely restricted, and he took pains to avoid anyone in the government or related to officials, for fear that he would be unmasked. There were relatively few people he could trust, and it was difficult to rely too frequently on their hospitality. As a result, his usual routine was to eat dinner in his room, supplementing his bread with an occasional cold joint. Fruits and vegetables were luxuries he could rarely afford.

Afraid to ask for credit from merchants who might discover his real identity and set the bailiffs on his trail again, he made almost no purchases. A lack of reading matter was the last straw, but Bentham again came to his rescue and made his library available to the refugee. Visiting Burr's room one day, the philosopher was shocked to find it was unbearably chilly, and the next morning the fugitive received a bag of coal as a gift from an anonymous admirer. Thereafter a similar bag was delivered each week.

During this enforced sojourn in London he made strenuous efforts to earn money; most of them were impractical, since he was unable to practice his own profession. He seemed to specialize in trying to sell the English rights for a number of French inventions, including a method for making false teeth and another for making vinegar at a price much lower than the process cost in England.

He also turned inventor himself. During his long months of idleness he had toyed with a design of his own for making a steamboat, and he worked hard on the blueprints, refining and changing them. A brief burst of optimism over the project was reminiscent of the old Aaron Burr. In a letter to Theodosia he declared that he had solved the problem of the steamboat, boasting that his creation could travel at a speed of twenty miles per hour and that with new improvements he had in mind, it would attain a maximum speed of thirty miles per hour. In other words, he explained, it would be possible to cross the Atlantic in six days instead of the three to five weeks achieved by the fastest seagoing sloops.

Even in his temporary elation, however, he wrote with a new note of caution. He was telling no one else his secret, he declared, and requested that Theodosia keep the matter to herself. In that way, he told her, he would not become a laughingstock again if unexpected difficulties prevented the completion of the project.

Work on his steamboat and the efforts to sell various other inventions occupied only a fraction of Burr's time. His chief concern was finding a ship that would take him back to the United States, but the obstacles in his path seemed insuperable. Not only did the war between Great Britain and France restrict transatlantic shipping, but on June 19, 1812, the United States would declare war on Britain. For all practical purposes the two nations were at war for many months prior to the formal declaration.

Meanwhile, American merchant ships avoided British ports and sea lanes because capture meant the vessels would be impounded, the seamen impressed into service in the British navy, and the officers sent into internment camps. A few daring American captains continued to sail between England and the New World, however, because their ships were registered under the flags of neutral countries. Such merchantmen offered Burr his best chance of escape; the only alternative to this means was to find a cargo brig that traveled between Britain and Canada.

On several occasions he succeeded in finding a merchant ship that would carry passengers across the Atlantic for a price. But their masters were shrewd, knowledgeable men, and two of them guessed the identity of the seedy "Adolphus Arnot" who applied to them for passage. He was vehement in his denials that he was actually Aaron Burr, but they preferred to take no chances, reasoning that neither the United States nor Britain would be pleased to learn that they had given transportation to a man who was sought by the authorities of both nations on a variety of charges.

Desperation led Burr to cast aside his caution, and he began to haunt the London waterfront, visiting taverns and inns, frequented by the officers and sailors of merchant ships that were anchored in the Thames. The possibility of arrest at any moment was always present, and time dragged on endlessly. Then, in early March, 1812, after an unavoidable stay of more than six months in London, Burr finally found a captain who was willing to take a few risks. The man was named Potter, and his brig, the *Aurora*, flew under the Swedish flag, making her a neutral vessel in the various wars that were upsetting the stability of the world. Captain Potter was an American, and the crew members remained on board the brig in port, which meant that in all probability they were also Americans. Burr guessed that Potter had no right to fly under the protection of the Swedish flag, but he did not care. Potter offered him passage, and nothing else mattered.

The offer was not unqualified, however. The usual price for a transatlantic crossing was ten pounds, but Potter demanded twenty pounds — in advance. This was a considerable sum, more than Burr dared to beg from Jeremy Bentham, and he had already exhausted his credit with virtually all of his other English acquaintances.

The situation was particularly critical because the *Aurora* was leaving London that same day on the afternoon tide; it would make a brief stop twenty-four hours later at Gravesend to take on water and last-minute provisions and would begin her transatlantic crossing at sundown. This meant Burr had almost no time to seek the necessary funds.

Alternate waves of exhilaration and despair washed over him. If he could obtain the necessary money, plus a small surplus to rent horses to carry him to Gravesend at a breakneck speed, he would be able to leave England within twenty-four hours. On the other hand, his mind was paralyzed by the gravity of his dilemma, and he could think of no one who would provide him with so large a sum.

For a precious hour he tramped the streets of London, deep in thought. Finally an idea occurred to him, born of his old audacity and an indifference to the fact that he would again have to humble himself. He had already suffered so many humiliations that one more did not matter, so he cast aside his pride and paid a visit to John Reeves at the Alien Office.

Reeves listened to Burr's story without interruption. At its conclusion he took three pounds from his purse and handed it to the American, confining himself to the remark that the money would pay for transportation to Gravesend. Then, not saying another word, he wrote a bank draft for twenty pounds and extended it across his desk.

Burr stammered his thanks and raced to the offices of Reeves's banker before they closed for the day. He completed the transaction shortly after sundown and literally ran back to his drab room to collect his few belongings, among them his precious Vanderlyn portrait of Theodosia, which he was able to carry in a single, small traveling case.

Escape at last was within reach, and the very idea made him dizzy as he dashed to the nearest table that rented post horses. Making his transaction there with all possible speed, he set out on his journey at once on a fog-shrouded, cold night. He paused only for a quick bite of food and a brief rest whenever he changed horses and reached Gravesend with approximately two hours to spare.

His mind had been racing in time to the beat of the horse's hooves, and before he joined the ship, he paused long enough to spend almost the last of his money on hair dye and a wig. Only then did he have himself rowed out to the *Aurora*, where he handed Captain Potter twenty pounds in cash.

The ship weighed anchor on time, and Aaron Burr sailed away toward an unknown future in the West, where he was wanted in a number of states on charges of murder, treason, conspiracy, and evasion of creditors. At the moment, however, he could not concern himself with such things. He was going home, and nothing else mattered.

Chapter 23

So many British warships were prowling the North Atlantic that the *Aurora* was forced to sail to the New World by a circuitous route, often changing course and sometimes doubling in her tracks. But Aaron Burr did not mind the long voyage; for the first time in several years he could eat as often and as much as he pleased, and long hours spent on the open deck restored a measure of his health and spirits.

He also amused himself by growing a beard, which he dyed a dark red to match his wig, and when the *Aurora* reached Boston in mid-May, 1812, he went ashore in disguise, his arrival in his native land unknown and unheralded. His habits of recent years were invaluable now as he took lodgings in a rooming house near the waterfront, where he called himself Mr. de Gamelli.

That same day he mailed two letters, hoping they would reach their destinations in less than the usual two to three months. The first went to Theodosia in Charleston, informing her of his safe arrival and rejoicing because he would soon be reunited with her and her child. The second went to his faithful crony in New York, Samuel Swartwout, whom he asked to make discreet inquiries concerning the charges that were still on the books against him.

The first reply came from Theodosia and shocked Aaron to the marrow. It said, in part:

> A few miserable days past, my dear father, and your late letter
> would have gladdened my soul: and even now I rejoice as
> much as it is possible for me to rejoice at anything; but there
> is no more joy for me; the world is a blank.

I have lost my boy. My child is gone forever. He expired on the 30th of June.

She included only a few details. Aaron Burr Alston had been stricken with what had appeared to be a head cold, but a fever had developed, and he had died within hours, though a battery of hastily summoned physicians had striven valiantly to save him.

The news stunned Burr. The thought of seeing his beloved daughter and grandson again had enabled him to survive during the long nightmare of his poverty-stricken existence in Paris and London, and it was difficult for him to believe that his grandson and namesake was gone. Realizing that Theodosia's loss was greater than his own, however, he rallied quickly and wrote her a tender letter, urging her to bear her sorrow with fortitude.

Then, still grieving, he received an eagerly awaited letter from Swartwout. The news from New York was better than he had any reason to expect. The state was willing to drop the murder charges against him, and only the claims of his creditors still marred his good name. Swartwout added that he had already held discussions with three or four major creditors, who were now inclined to give Colonel Burr the chance to make good his debts and indicated that for the present they would not press charges against him. Once the details were settled, Swartwout declared, other creditors would be almost certain to fall into line. He therefore deemed it safe for his old friend and patron to return to New York for the purpose of reassuring the more important creditors himself, and extended an invitation to live under his own roof.

Relieved beyond measure to put his anonymous existence behind him, Burr sold several of his remaining belongings so he could pay his rooming-house bill, then caught the stagecoach for New York City. He arrived there on June 7, 1812, four years to the day after his departure. Reaching the city after dark, he proceeded on foot, his face shaded by a broad-brimmed hat, to Swartwout's house on Stone Street. The negotiations with the various creditors were opened the following morning, and Burr did his earned best to convince them that he wanted only the opportunity to repay every penny he owed them so he could once again walk with his head held high.

Meanwhile, without his knowledge, Theodosia roused herself from her sorrow-induced lethargy to help him. Burr's old friend and college mate, James Madison, was now President of the United States, and Theodosia, needing no one to tell her that the First Lady had always been fond of her father, wrote to Dolley Madison for assistance. She also sent a similar, somewhat shorter letter to Secretary of the Treasury Albert Gallatin. However, he had gone off to Europe in May as the President's representative in negotiations that, had they been completed, would have enabled Russia to act as a mediator between the United States and Great Britain. Only Gallatin's absence from the country prevented him from taking action on Burr's behalf.

But no assistance other than Dolley Madison's was needed. She showed Theodosia's letter to her husband, and the President remembered many things: He recalled the brilliant promise Aaron Burr had shown as a young man, and he could not forget that he owed his own marital happiness to Aaron Burr. His time and attention fully occupied by the war the still-weak United States was waging against Great Britain, President Madison nevertheless felt deep pity for the once-dangerous lion, now impotent, penniless, and bereft of political influence.

Acting quietly and unofficially, the President passed a few words to key subordinates, while the First Lady was able to write to Theodosia, assuring her that the federal government intended to take no action against Colonel Burr. She hastened to add that the failure of the federal government to press charges might not have any influence on the several states that had not quashed their own charges against him. Theodosia relayed the good news to her father.

In the meantime, Burr's negotiations with his creditors in New York had been completely successful. These men, acting in concert, had agreed to take no action against him provided he began to make financial reparations within six months and made regular payments thereafter until all of his debts were wiped out. An informal agreement was signed, and although Burr could not travel to many other states for fear of being imprisoned, he was free to emerge from the shadows into the open in New York.

On July 5, 1812, he rented a small suite of rooms at 9 Nassau Street, in the heart of New York's business and commercial district, and advertised his presence with a sedate, inconspicuous sign that read:

Aaron Burr

Attorney-at-Law

Nothing better illustrates the changing temper of the United States than the fact that Aaron Burr's return failed to create even a ripple of excitement. A few, scattered newspapers printed brief articles regarding his reappearance, but no one seemed to care. So much had happened since he had gone off to England that most people regarded the killing of Alexander Hamilton and the later conspiracy and treason trial as ancient history. The war with Britain and the problems of earning a living occupied the attention of most citizens, others were concerning themselves with the rapid growth of the West, and the thousands of British and European immigrants who were arriving each year had never heard of the notorious Colonel Burr.

Those who did remember him were prominent businessmen and chieftains of the Tammany Society, all of whom recalled that there had been no better lawyer in New York. Regardless of what men might think of him as a private individual, they were eager to be represented by someone of his acumen and skill in thorny legal cases. So, somewhat to Burr's own surprise, clients began to flock to his office, and in the first two weeks after he reopened his practice, he earned the enormous sum of more than two thousand dollars.

Perhaps the greatest of miracles was the fact that he kept his word to his creditors, paying them more than half of his initial income. Thereafter, as the money continued to roll in, he remained faithful to his obligations until, over a period of several years, he managed to pay back every penny he owed.

Some of Burr's early biographers attribute these actions to a change of heart and claim that he had reformed as a result of his sobering experiences abroad. But his journal, which he continued to keep, offers positive proof that other motives were responsible. His creditors had forgiven him only to the extent that they were giving him the chance to repay his debts, and they were keeping him under close surveillance. Any attempt to cheat them, any failure to pay, would cause them to file new charges. He was weary of flight, poverty, and the inability to earn a living at anything other than the law, so it was easier to remain in New York, work as an attorney, and satisfy his creditors.

His sojourn in Europe had taught him to live simply, and his wants were relatively few. His success enabled him to rent rooms on Nassau Street above his law offices. There he established a small apartment that consisted of a comfortable sitting room, a small bedchamber, an equally small dining room, and an adequate kitchen. He hired a combination housemaid-cook to keep the place clean, attend to his laundry, shop for provisions, and prepare his simple meals.

He bought new clothes to replace the threadbare outfits that had seen such long service, but he indulged in no extravagances. Indigestion continued to plague him, so he ate simple meals and rarely drank anything other than coffee and a small glass of watered wine with his meals. He rarely entertained, he no longer had a grandson on whom he could lavish gifts, and books were his only extravagance. His other expenses were few, and as a consequence, he saved large sums of money, not because of any particular desire to save, but because he had no reason to indulge in heavy spending. He was therefore able to pay off his debts much sooner than either he or his delighted creditors had anticipated.

Above all else, he wanted to see Theodosia, but it was dangerous for him to travel because a number of states had not yet withdrawn their indictments against him. Accordingly, he urged his daughter to come to New York, assuring her that the rest, the change of scene, and the solace he could offer her after their long separation would be beneficial and soothing to her.

Theodosia agreed to make the trip, even though the prospect of traveling alone in such disturbed times did not appeal to her. Her husband could not accompany her because he had recently been elected Governor of South Carolina and consequently held the post of Commander-in-Chief of the state's militia, which might be called to federal duty at any time.

Since overland travel would be fatiguing to a woman already suffering from emotional exhaustion, Burr urged her to come by sea, stressing that a voyage on a ship that hugged the coast would be safe and offering to send an escort to accompany her. The idea appealed to Theodosia, so he made the necessary arrangements with an elderly friend, Dr. Timothy Greene, a widower with lots of free time.

Dr. Greene made the journey to Charleston and discovered that although Theodosia was in a state of semi-collapse, she was still determined to visit her father. Burr, meanwhile, had badly underestimated the dangers of sea travel. A squadron of swift, heavily armed British frigates and sloops was blockading the Atlantic ports of the United States, and all American shipping was considered legitimate prey.

Governor Alston rose to that emergency on his wife's behalf. First he rented a schooner for her, a sleek ship called the *Patriot*. Then, the age of chivalry not yet having come to an end, he sent off a letter on another schooner, the *Charleston*, to Sir Alexander Cochrane, the commander of the British squadron. In it he explained that his wife, who had recently lost her only child, was traveling to New York for the purpose of visiting her father, whom Alston did not name, and he asked the admiral to show every possible courtesy of the sea to the bereaved first lady of South Carolina.

Accompanied by Dr. Greene, Theodosia Burr Alston sailed from Charleston on December 30. Her husband, several members of his family, and a number of friends escorted her to the chartered ship.

Ordinarily a vessel of the *Patriot*'s size would have made the voyage from Charleston to New York in seven to ten days but might have been forced to remain at sea for as long as two weeks. Early in January a storm off Cape Hatteras, North Carolina, had made it necessary for the blockading British fleet to put far out to sea, and a worried Aaron Burr at first assumed that the captain of the *Patriot*, an experienced ship's master, had done the same. But his concern turned to alarm when the schooner failed to appear after three weeks.

In February the news of Theodosia Burr Alston's disappearance was printed in the Charleston press, and within a few days Burr once again found himself in the headlines. The newspapers — and the American public — speculated endlessly on the fate of the first lady of South Carolina, who was of even greater interest to the world because she was the daughter of the notorious, controversial Aaron Burr.

According to the most persistent rumors, the *Patriot* had been captured by the British, and Theodosia either had been taken to Bermuda or was being held captive on the high seas. Some of the more belligerent newspapers went so far as to declare that the enemy was holding her for ransom.

It was also said on equally flimsy authority that the *Patriot* had been smashed to kindling in a storm, and bits of wreckage that washed ashore at various places on the Atlantic coastline, from Maine and Massachusetts to the Floridas, were offered as proof of this assertion. This story gave rise to another flood of rumors: Theodosia was the only survivor and was recovering her health in some small coastal hamlet. Either she was unable to speak and consequently could not identify herself, or she was suffering from amnesia. Presumably the residents of the village did not know who she was, either.

According to the most exotic of the rumors, Theodosia had been captured by coastal pirates, some of whom made their headquarters on Hispaniola or other West Indian islands.

These fanciful accounts asserted that she had been taken into concubinage by a buccaneer. The mere mention of pirates opened a new line of speculation, and it was said that Theodosia, her maid, and Dr. Greene had either been thrown into the sea or been forced to walk the plank.

Aaron Burr, suffering the worst of blows in a life that had been plagued by misfortune, refused to grant interviews and maintained a tight-lipped silence. Governor Alston also refused to speak for publication, but by early March the continuing speculation compelled him to call in the press, and he offered a reward of ten thousand dollars in silver to anyone who could bring him positive proof of his wife's fate.

The promise of such a large sum stirred the interest and greed of fortune-hunters and cranks, and for months Alston was plagued by letters and personal visits from men and women who swore they were in possession of the proof he required. A few of the many leads sounded vaguely promising, and all of them were followed but without success.

The military catastrophes suffered by the United States in her war with the British caused a sharp increase in the American public's hatred of Great Britain, so newspaper and magazine publishers, pamphleteers, and others fanned the flames by keeping alive the story that Theodosia had been captured by Sir Alexander Cochrane or one of his subordinates. The rumor gained such credence that Burr, who had no reason to be fond of Great Britain, nevertheless deemed it necessary to call a halt to the publication of such nonsense.

He issued a brief statement, saying, "The Royal Navy does not make war on defenseless women."

That ended the absurd talk, and he retreated to grieve in private. Never had he known such deep, abiding sorrow; neither the loss of his wife nor any of his other tragedies had caused him so much pain. His love for his daughter had been the core of his life, and only that love had sustained him through the long, poverty-stricken years of his exile. Her disappearance robbed him of what little joy he was still capable of feeling.

Chapter 24

The death of Theodosia was responsible for a major change in the public's attitude toward Aaron Burr, and the wave of sympathy that swept across the country washed away the revulsion that had still been felt everywhere. Prominent citizens continued to refuse to invite him to their homes, and there were many who did not hesitate to snub him when they encountered him on the street, but the common man did not share these sentiments. Crowds gathered outside a tavern when it became known he was dining there, people stared at him whenever he was recognized in public, and it was not unusual for groups to wait patiently outside his office-home on Nassau Street for a glimpse of him.

The tragedy restored him to the limelight he had taken for granted prior to his treason trial and departure into exile, and he remained an exciting figure until the end of his days. People were curious about him, and although there were few who truly liked him, he had already become a legend. He was aware of the people's interest, and that knowledge gave him what little satisfaction he knew in the many years he continued to live.

His vanity compelled him to play his new role to the hilt. Dressing impeccably, as he had done for so many years prior to his exile, he made it his habit to take a long walk late every afternoon, regardless of the weather. His limp had become permanent, but it did not deter him, and his stride was arrogant, almost jaunty. He stared straight ahead, seeing no one, and rarely recognized gentlemen of his acquaintance. But he was always gallant to ladies whom he knew, removing his hat and bowing to them when they passed in their carriages.

Even in private his manner was aloof. His law business continued to flourish, and by the time the war ended in 1814 he had managed to pay off most of his debts. He was strictly impersonal in his dealings with his clients, confining his discussions to the legal business at hand. Occasionally someone tried to draw him into personal conversation, but he invariably rebuffed these attempts and erected an invisible shield that placed a distance between him and the people with whom he dealt.

Occasionally a visitor invited him to a dinner party or reception, breaking through the unspoken boycott of those who still branded him as a pariah, but he politely refused. He never offered an explanation, and his seeming isolation made him a mysterious figure, a romantic conceit that he also enjoyed.

His law practice grew, and he found it necessary to hire several clerks. When his Nassau Street offices became inadequate, he moved to larger quarters on Reade Street. There he selected the darkest room of the suite for his office, his clerks believing the choice was motivated by his conviction that it contributed to his reputation as a man of mystery. No matter how completely he might he avoided socially by the aristocrats and upper-middleclass men of New York, no one could deny that he had few equals as an attorney, as his victories in court and in private negotiations on behalf of his clients testified. Accordingly many young lawyers and law students were anxious to enter his employ.

His staff usually consisted of two or three associates and one or two clerks. He treated them with the same severity he displayed to the outside world, never unbending, never engaging in personal conversation. Thirty to forty young men worked for him over the years, and at no time did he speak to any one of them on a subject other than the law. He was so remote, in fact, that some of them resigned, claiming he harbored no real human feelings.

Regardless of his contemporaries' reaction to him, no one dared to insult him to his face. Aside from his daily walks, the only recreation in which he indulged was his thirty-minute practice with pistols early every morning, and his clerks let it be known that he was still an unerringly expert shot. His targets were outlines of a man's figure, drawn on heavy paper and pinned to a tree, and his young associates, who collected them after his practice and saved them as mementos, frequently showed them to people. Several of them, punctured by bullet holes in the heart and other vital organs, are still extant more than a century and a half later.

It is possible that Burr maintained the routine of target practice for purposes of possible self-defense rather than for sport. He was aware than many men still actively disliked him, but he made certain that no one dared to insult or vilify him in his hearing.

He habitually carried a pistol in a pocket of his tailcoat when he left his office-home, and an incident that took place in May, 1817, illustrates that his caution was justified. According to the accounts of several witnesses, he journeyed to Westchester County, outside New York City, in connection with a case he was handling and stopped at a small country inn for dinner on his way home. He was recognized, and before he completed his meal a group of men entered the place, threatening to kill him.

Burr immediately drew his pistol. Then, speaking in a quiet, conversational tone, he made these self-appointed enemies an offer. He expressed a willingness to meet any one of them — without delay — in a duel behind the inn. If they chose to reject his offer, however, he promised to kill the first man who raised a hand against him. His foes instantly changed their minds and departed, leaving him in peace.

According to the correspondence of a number of contemporaries, Burr managed to stave off possible confrontations with other individuals who had expressed an eagerness to "teach him a lesson." When such people called on him and he became conscious of their hostility and sensed that they were looking for a reason to provoke a fight, he usually found a way to make a casual reference to "my friend Hamilton, whom I shot." His manner on such occasions was so impersonal that the blood of the hotheads cooled very quickly.

Only one prominent American whom Burr encountered is known to have refused to shake his hand. One day, in a New York courtroom, he offered his hand to Henry Clay, of Kentucky, the leader of the Whig party in Congress and one of the most active of the younger generation of American statesmen. Clay merely stared at him, turned on his heel, and stalked away. Had he spoken the thoughts that were obviously in his mind, by-standers declared, the impassive Colonel Burr undoubtedly would have called him out.

What the world at large did not know — and even the few of his old cronies who saw him from time to time did not suspect — was that Burr carried on an active social life. He never recovered from the shock of Theodosia's disappearance, and his bedchamber, which no outsider saw, was filled with mementos, trinkets, and framed letters she had sent him. Those reminders of his daughter did not assuage his loneliness, however, and each day, after the departure of the members of his staff, he retired to his living quarters above his office and engaged in his very private social life.

Only his maid-cook knew his secret, and she told it to no one. The truth of the matter was that Aaron Burr entertained extensively and philanthropically. He made it his business to find deserving girls and boys whose families were too poor to provide them with an education, and then he became acquainted with them by inviting them and their parents to a long series of dinners. After spending six months in the company of a child and his parents, he secretly paid for the young person's higher education.

He kept only fragmentary records of this aid, which has come to posterity's attention only because of the letters these young people wrote to him. At least four young men were assisted in this manner, two of them attending his own school, Princeton, the others attending Yale. Three young women are known to have taken lessons in French, the classics, music, and deportment, and their education was completed by trips abroad, accompanied by their parents. All three, if their correspondence is any criterion, subsequently married men of substance.

Burr derived deep, personal satisfaction from these activities. His small dinner parties banished his loneliness, at least for a few hours; by acting as a surrogate father he could compensate, to a minor degree, for the irrevocable loss of his daughter. It has been suggested, too, that he may have been motivated by a lifetime of accumulated guilts, which could have prompted him to sponsor a worthy cause, but there is no evidence to substantiate this opinion. At no time, either in his actions or in his words, did Burr even hint that his misdeed caused him to feel as much as a twinge of remorse.

One other factor may have contributed to his philanthropy. His continuing success as an attorney was undiminished, and he earned an annual income as great as that of any other professional man in New York, but he had no one to whom he could give his money. His wife's children by her previous marriage were successful in their own right and had no need of his assistance; his sister's children were comfortably situated, too, and he had no other direct heirs. He no longer pursued a spendthrift existence, and although he continued to set a lavish table for his few guests, his own needs were few. His clothes were expensive, but he seldom needed to add to his extensive wardrobe, and his only extravagance was his purchase of books. His library was reputedly one of the largest in the city, but he was generous to a fault, and when one of his young guests displayed an enthusiasm for literature, he sometimes gave the boy or girl hundreds of his books.

In 1820 he adopted a six-year-old orphan named Charles Burdett, and the child lived with him until late adolescence, when he left home to become a midshipman in the United States Navy. Many years later Captain Burdett wrote his reminiscences of Aaron Burr. The document was a loving tribute to a foster father who had been devoted to his welfare and education.

In the early 1820s there were other additions to the household. A widow from Connecticut, Mrs. Medcef Eden, who was a friend of Burr's cousins there, asked him to represent her in a lawsuit involving a small inheritance. He won the case for her, and soon thereafter Mrs. Eden accepted employment as his housekeeper, bringing with her two young daughters, Rebecca and Elizabeth. Burr treated the girls as his own children, and Mrs. Eden stayed with him until both were married. He gave each of the girls generous gifts when they went off to establish their own households.

Old friends were not forgotten or ignored, either. In 1822 Luther Martin, who had represented Burr with such success at his treason trial, came to New York. He was penniless, his health impaired by his drinking, and having incurred the disgust and enmity of relatives and friends in Baltimore, he had nowhere else to go.

Burr took him in, summoned a competent physician, and thereafter helped nurse Martin back to relatively good health. It was impossible for the old man to earn a living, so Burr gave him a permanent home under his own roof and enabled him to find a reason for living by pretending to consult him on difficult legal matters, although Martin's advancing senility rendered his advice worthless. He lived with Burr for four years, until his death in 1826.

The success Burr enjoyed in his practice was due, in part, to his willingness to handle any case, including the type that attorneys who guarded their reputations zealously were inclined to shun. He represented both plaintiffs and defendants in various spectacular divorce cases, and on many occasions he was hired by men accused of having earned large sums of money in shady ways.

Some of New York's more prominent lawyers were inclined to look down their noses at Colonel Burr in public, but they did not hesitate to go to him in private — and pay him substantial consultation fees — when they were involved in cases requiring a detailed knowledge of the intricate fine points of law. No one knew the law better than he, and no one was more adept at winning supposedly hopeless cases.

Governor Alston remained loyal to his father-in-law and to the memory of the lost Theodosia. In 1815 and again in 1819 the South Carolinian wrote to Burr, asking if he needed any financial assistance. On both occasions Burr thanked him for his kindness, then assured him that he was earning more than he needed.

One old vice remained. It was impossible for Burr to avoid the temptation of speculating in western lands. Each time he put money into a new company he expressed the certainty that his small investment would earn an enormous fortune. He invariably lost every penny but refused to learn from his unhappy experiences and continued to make such investments until he reached the age of seventy-five.

It must be emphasized that he had no ulterior motive in sinking funds into land companies. The combination of Theodosia's tragic disappearance and his own poverty-stricken years in England and France had robbed him of all desire for adventure. He had abandoned his dream of empire and neither revived it nor substituted another for it. In the last quarter century of his life he became a hard-headed realist who kept his imagination in check.

He had sources of income other than his law practice that made it possible for him, as he grew older, to devote fewer hours to his work. Many years earlier he had purchased an annuity in England, and in 1826, when he was seventy, he was paid an annual sum. Two years earlier he applied for a pension as a veteran of the War of Independence, and it won automatic approval, so he began to receive regular monthly payments in 1828.

When Andrew Jackson became President of the United States in 1828, the post of Secretary of State went to Martin Van Buren, of New York, whom Burr had known since his entry into politics many years earlier. Samuel Swartwout and other Burr cronies received high federal appointments, and

Burr showed a trace of his old spark by making an attempt to cut in on the spoils himself. A scant six weeks after President Jackson took office he applied to the government for the sum of $100,000, claiming he had spent the money out of his own pocket during the War of Independence.

It was true, of course, that he had purchased uniforms, muskets, ammunition, and food for his regiment and that he had never received repayment. Whether he had actually spent as much as he claimed, however, was dubious.

His claim was brusquely rejected, but he was offered no explanation. The matter was mentioned casually in conversation prior to the beginning of a Cabinet meeting in the White House, and the President, who had just entered the room, heard the talk. Andrew Jackson had a long, sharp memory and announced in no uncertain terms, "I shall discharge any man who pays a single penny to that arch-traitor!" The War Department acted accordingly, and Secretary of State Van Buren did not feel disposed to enter into battle on Colonel Burr's behalf.

As the years fled by, Burr lost what little remained of his handsome appearance. He grew completely bald except for a thin fringe of white, and his bulging forehead made him look top-heavy. There were few wrinkles in his face, but his skin was drawn taut over his bones, and many people remarked on his resemblance to a skeleton. His bearing was erect, however, and his walk remained brisk, even though the limp was more pronounced.

Though his indigestion bothered him from time to time, he suffered from no other physical complaints except insomnia, and he attributed his vigor to his moderation in eating and drinking. His only major vice was smoking, and he was seldom without one of the long black *segaros* he cherished. He did not begin to use spectacles for reading until he was sixty-eight, and until the end of his days he needed glasses only for reading.

His mind was as sharp as that of men half his age, and when complicated legal matters required his attention, he could concentrate on them for hours at a time. The wicked, President Jackson said, were a resilient breed. Then, abruptly, in 1830 the situation changed.

Chapter 25

On the afternoon of June 17, 1830, when Aaron Burr was seventy-four years of age, he was seated at his desk in his office, writing a legal brief, when he suddenly toppled forward and fell unconscious. A physician, hastily summoned, said he had suffered a stroke. A cousin, Kate Hawes, nursed him back to health, remaining with him for almost two months, and shared his relief when the attack proved minor. He emerged from the ordeal with all of his faculties unimpaired and resumed the life he had been leading prior to his illness.

But the physical warning that he was mortal, like other men, had its effect on him, and he began to make frequent trips to Princeton, where he was seen visiting the graves of his father, mother, and grandfather. He also paid a number of visits to Princeton College but was not surprised when the officials of the school ignored his presence. He was accustomed to snubs from men in high places, but the undergraduates who were members of the Cliosophic Society he had headed in his own student days knew little of his lurid past and cared less. Most of them had not been born when he had been tried for treason, and to them he was a glamorous, important figure.

Twice they invited him to attend their annual dinner. On both occasions he was the presiding officer, making graceful little speeches and acting as toastmaster. In 1831 he bought the two volume dictionary prepared by Noah Webster and presented it to the society with his compliments.

Then, in 1832, Aaron Burr hit the newspaper headlines again with the last of his spectacular exploits. When he had been Vice-President, he had known a young woman by the name of

Eliza Bowen from Rhode Island, whose company had been much in demand on social occasions. Eliza had begun life as a streetwalker and then became a courtesan who was supported by wealthy men. There had been gossip about a possible romance, but the relationship had withered, presumably because the Vice-President had been concentrating on his ambitious scheme to establish his own nation in the West.

Subsequently Miss Bowen had married the wealthy Stephen Jumel, of New York. Now she was a widow who owned shares in a number of prosperous companies and was the mistress of a large, handsome mansion in Washington Heights, just outside New York City. Twenty years younger than Aaron, she was still strikingly attractive and wore her clothes with an air that caused a stir wherever she went.

How and when her path again crossed that of Aaron Burr is not known, but early in 1832 he began to pay court to her, pressing his suit with the intensity of a young bachelor. It has been supposed that he was drawn to her because she was both wealthy and attractive, but no one knows why Eliza became interested in a man of seventy-five. According to contemporary rumors that have never been verified, Eliza was greedy; not satisfied with the fortune she already possessed, she wanted to add to it and supposedly believed that Burr had accumulated vast sums since his return from exile.

The motives of Aaron and Eliza are as much of a mystery today as they were in 1832 and 1833, but the facts speak for themselves: Mrs. Eliza Bowen Jumel, widow, and Colonel Aaron Burr, widower, were married in 1833 by a justice of the peace. They went off in the bride's magnificently appointed carriage for a honeymoon in New England before settling down together in the Jumel mansion, and the gossips enjoyed a new feast. Stories about Burr and his bride appeared in dozens of newspapers, and all of the old scandals about the seventy-seven-year-old bridegroom again were aired in print. Ribald songs and poems were written about the couple, and the few men still living who remembered Burr's first wife called him an old fool.

The marriage was turbulent from the outset. Burr insisted that his wife sell six thousand dollars' worth of shares in a Hartford construction company to pay the expenses of their honeymoon, and when she balked, he arranged the transaction himself. The rights of women were severely restricted in the 1830s, and a married man had every legal right to act in his wife's behalf, so there was literally nothing Eliza could do to prevent the sale of the stock.

Burr reverted to the habits of earlier years and overnight became a spendthrift. In less than two months he not only spent the six thousand dollars, but sold more of Eliza's securities for another seven thousand, then squandered that money, too. The furious bride went to war, and fifty-three days after the marriage Burr left the Jumel mansion and returned to the apartment above his office.

A few weeks later he suffered a second stroke, somewhat milder than the first, but sufficiently severe to confine him to his bed. Eliza still felt affectionate toward him because she appeared at his apartment with two manservants, who carried him to her coach and transported him back to her mansion. There she nursed him, and a month late the was his old self, dapper and audacious, showing no ill effects of his ailment and no signs of remorse.

He immediately reverted to the habits he had formed on their honeymoon and spent Eliza's money with reckless, joyous abandon. He sent expensive gifts to Burdett and other former wards, bought himself two or three complete new wardrobes, and invested heavily in a land company whose stock was virtually worthless.

The firey Eliza did not accept these spendthrift gestures meekly, and the gossips of New York learned, through the Burr servants, that the couple fought at breakfast, at dinner, and every evening. All that prevented arguments during the day was Burr's absence, since he traveled to his office every morning and did not return home until sunset. He always rode in one of the Jumel coaches, using them as though they were his own.

The expected climax came in the autumn of 1834, a little more than a year after the couple had been married, when Eliza discovered he was involved in one, and possibly two, extramarital affairs. Burr left the Jumel mansion for the last time, taking his belongings with him to his apartment, and Eliza immediately sued him for divorce. He wasted no time filing a countersuit brimming with legal complications.

Eliza perpetrated a master stroke that would have devastated a more sensitive opponent by hiring Alexander Hamilton, Jr., as her attorney.

The press erupted again when preliminary hearings were held early in 1835. The younger Hamilton appeared as the attorney for the defense, and the seventy-nine-year-old Aaron Burr represented himself. Both parties made so many charges, financial as well as personal, that the court took the case under advisement, requesting both sides to submit substantiating material within a period of six months, and reserved judgment, making it clear that no final decision would be rendered for at least a year. It may have been the court's desire to wait until the publicity flurry died away before holding another hearing.

Burr went back to the style of living he had followed prior to his marriage, but as he approached his eightieth birthday, he discovered he could no longer handle the volume of his law business alone, so he took in a partner named Croft. Soon thereafter the old man suffered a stroke that paralyzed his left leg and partly paralyzed his left arm. He could no longer walk and had to be carried downstairs from his bedroom to his office.

It soon became evident that he was unable to continue working efficiently, and it was equally obvious that he needed constant care. Croft hired a lady in reduced circumstances, a Mrs. Newton, to look after him, and Burr was moved into a suite in a genteel boardinghouse that she maintained. Croft now took complete charge of the law office, but he honored his financial commitment to Burr and paid all of his bills for room, board, medical assistance, and nursing care.

Burr, meanwhile, was still receiving his English annuity and his United States Army pension, so he used this money to buy more books. Refusing to admit that his life was drawing to a close, he insisted on maintaining the heavy schedule he had observed for years and read at least four or five books each week. His physicians humored him, telling Mrs. Newton that the books could do him no harm: They kept him occupied and prevented him from brooding about his failing health.

Samuel Swartwout and Matthew Davis were daily visitors to the sickroom, and a few other old cronies called occasionally. Ogden Edwards, a cousin, came to see him frequently, and Kate Hawes came, too. Burr received his visitors cheerfully, showing no sign of depression because his end was drawing close. One last, major problem remained to be settled, and he husbanded his energy for the task.

Designating Davis as his official biographer, he spent hours each day with his old friend, reminiscing about the past and occasionally writing brief notes as reminders of material he wanted included in the biography. Of primary importance, he said, was the complete record of his military activities; he remained convinced that he had been a genius and that only Washington's opposition had prevented him from winning universal recognition.

He charged Davis with the task of "telling the truth" about Washington. He also made it plain that he believed he could have captured Quebec in 1775 had he, rather than Benedict Arnold, been in command of the American expedition. His memory played deliberate tricks as he tried hard to justify his activities in the West. Omitting any mention of his dealings with the British and Spanish ministers to the United States, he claimed repeatedly that everything he had done, everything he had planned, had been done for the benefit and glory of his native country. His basic idea, he declared, had been to conquer Mexico and then annex it to the United States.

Thanks to one of history's stranger coincidences, American settlers who had been moving into the Mexican province of Texas revolted in the autumn of 1835, establishing a provisional government in November of that year and declaring their independence a few months later. This news was duly reported to Burr by his old friends, and he felt that history had vindicated him. He had envisaged precisely the events that were now taking place, he said, and had stood almost alone in his attempts to win the independence of Texas and then annex the country. Because other, lesser men had lacked his vision, they had persecuted him, tried him for treason, blackened his name, and forced him to suffer countless hardships. But now, in his final days, he believed, his reputation emerged unsullied at last, and he predicted that the day was not far distant when a free Texas would petition the United States for admission into the Union as a state.

In December, 1835, Davis brought Burr a copy of the first biography written about him. Its author was Samuel L. Knapp, whom he had met on only a few occasions. It was a slovenly work, inaccurate and incomplete. But it was a sentimental tale, highly favorable to its subject, so Burr made no objection to its errors, and he told Ogden Edwards he was content in the knowledge that posterity would judge him as he should be judged.

In the early spring of 1836, a short time after Burr's eightieth birthday, Mrs. Newton's lease on her house expired, and she was forced to take another place nearby. Burr did not move with her. Instead, he had himself removed to the little village of Port Richmond on Staten Island, where several members of the Edwards family lived. He told Samuel Swartwout that Mrs. Newton was "a good woman, too good for my comfort." She was so concerned about his immortal soul, he confided, that she had been badgering him in an attempt to persuade him to join a church before he died. He had no intention of taking any such step, he said, as it would have made a mockery of his whole life. So rather than hurt Mrs. Newton's feelings, he preferred to end his days elsewhere than under her roof.

He took lodgings in a place called Winants Inn, and his health was sufficiently good for him to be carried down to the dining room every evening for dinner in the spring and early summer of 1836. Most of the other guests were young United States Navy officers and their wives, and Burr enjoyed their company as much as they relished his.

Soon the other residents of the hotel were doing special favors for the old man. The officers ran errands, bringing him books he ordered and sometimes going to Manhattan to buy small quantities of a particularly delicate custard he enjoyed. The navy wives took turns reading to him when he wanted to rest his eyes, and he was especially partial to one pretty girl who reminded him of Theodosia.

One afternoon, in a rare expression of his innermost feelings, he confided to her that only two people on earth had ever meant anything to him — his first wife and their daughter. He had been ambitious in the years before his marriage to Theodosia Prevost, to be sure, but their mutual love had given his yearnings new meaning, and until her death he had wanted to achieve greatness only for her sake. Thereafter he had transferred his feelings and had striven for immortality because of his daughter.

"I wanted her to be proud of me," he said.

Almost a quarter of a century had passed since her death, but he still missed her, and his life had been meaningless since her loss. He didn't believe in life after death, he said, but he admitted the possibility of its existence, and for that reason he was reconciled to his passing.

"Either I shall move into an eternal void, knowing nothing," he declared, "or I shall be reunited with the two whom I love. Either way I am content."

By the middle of the summer his condition became worse, and he could no longer leave his bed. By this time the navy officers and their wives were so fond of him that they crowded into his room, and his physicians found it necessary to restrict their visits.

A number of clergymen showed great interest in Burr during the spring and summer of 1836, but most of them were so eager to convert him to their various brands of Christianity that he dismissed them with scant courtesy. One who took a more subtle approach was the Reverend Dr. P. J. Van Pelt, a Dutch Reformed minister, who managed to establish a friendly relationship with the old man. They discussed theology by the hour, and Burr was always lucid, his mind quite keen as he defended his own free-thinking position. He quietly resisted Dr. Van Pelt's attempts to convert him, saying that if God knew of his existence and cared what became of him, a change of heart at the eleventh hour would not convince the Almighty that he was sincere in his abandonment of his lifelong beliefs.

But he was deeply touched by the minister's prayers for him and always thanked him for them. One afternoon in August when they were having a discussion, the chambermaid entered the room to give Burr a dose of the medicine the physicians had prescribed for him. He was engrossed in his talk with Dr. Van Pelt and waved the woman away, but she refused to leave until he took the bitter-tasting medicine.

"Go to hell," Burr told her.

She replied that she had been in communication with the devil and that he had informed her he was intending to welcome Colonel Burr in the near future, so there would be no room in hell for anyone else. Burr laughed heartily, and Dr. Van Pelt later reported that nothing in his attitude indicated fear of his impending end.

In the first days of September he began to fail, and Dr. Van Pelt made more strenuous efforts to persuade him to accept God, but he continued to resist. On September 13 it was apparent to the attending physicians that the end was near, and Dr. Van Pelt remained with Burr through the long night. A few moments after daybreak the clergyman gently asked the dying man if he was prepared to accept salvation.

Burr looked up, a glint of humor in his still-magnetic eyes. "On that subject I am coy," he said, consistent to the last. A few moments later he fell asleep, and that afternoon, at 2:00, he expired quietly.

Dr. Van Pelt conducted a memorial service at the hotel for relatives and friends, and Burr, in accordance with his wish, was buried beside his parents and grandfather in Princeton. On September 16 the student body of Princeton College, led by members of the Cliosophic Society, marched to the cemetery behind a military band, and Dr. James Carnahan, the president of the college, delivered a brief funeral oration, discreetly making no mention of the turbulent events in Aaron Burr's life.

The sun had been shining earlier in the day, but threatening clouds filled the sky during the service, and when the gravediggers began to fill in the hole in which the coffin had been placed, a sudden deluge turned the dry earth to mud.

Afterword

Aaron Burr, alternately sentimentalized and pilloried by historians for a century and a half, has had the last laugh at the expense of posterity. Many of the details of his life are still surrounded by mystery, and the full story of his elaborate conspiracy has never become fully known. Even the modern biographer must fit together the pieces of the puzzle, knowing that some are still missing.

It is difficult to avoid the temptation to think that Aaron Burr would have relished the continuing controversy over various aspects of his spectacular life.

In passing, let me note that Commodore Thomas Truxton, U.S.N., spelled his surname in two ways, often changing the final vowel from *o* to *u*. I have arbitrarily chosen the former, although it was the less commonly used in his own time, because a majority of the various branches of the Truxton family use that spelling today.

N.B.G.

New York City

Selected Bibliography

MANUSCRIPTS

American Antiquarian Society: Burr Papers

Connecticut Historical Society: Burr Papers; Jefferson Papers

Harvard University: Burr Papers

J. P. Morgan Library: Burr Papers

Library of Congress: Conspiracy Papers; Burr Miscellaneous
  Papers; Hamilton Papers; Jefferson Papers

New Jersey Historical Society: Burr Papers

New York Historical Society: Burr Papers; Gallatin Papers

New York Public Library: Burr Papers; Madison Papers

New York State Library: Burr Papers

Princeton University Library: Burr Papers

PRINTED SOURCES

Adams, George. *Sketch of Aaron Burr.* New York, 1876.

Alexander, D. S. *Political History of New York,* New York, 1906.
  4 vols.

Alexander, Holmes. *Aaron Burr, the Proud Pretender,* New York,
  1937.

Beveridge, Albert J. *The Life of John Marshall.* Boston, 1916. 4
  vols.

Biddle, Charles. *Autobiography.* Philadelphia, 1883.

Bowers, Claude G. *Jefferson and Hamilton.* Boston, 1926.

Burdett, Charles. *Reminiscences of Aaron Burr,* New York, 1858.

Carpenter, T. *Reports on the Trials of Aaron Burr.* Washington,
  D.C., 1808. 3 vols.

Clark, A. C. *Life and Letters of Dolley Madison.* Washington, D.C.,
  1814.

Davis, Matthew L. *Memoirs of Aaron Burr*. New York, 1836. 2 vols.

——, ed. *Burr's Private Journal*. New York, 1858. 2 vols.

Duncan, William C. *The Amazing Madame Jumel*. New York, 1935.

Fitzpatrick, J. C. *Writings of Washington*. Washington, D.C., 1931-1944. 39 vols.

Ford, H. J. *Alexander Hamilton*. New York, 1920.

Ford, Worthington C. *Some Papers of Aaron Burr*. Worcester, Mass., 1920.

James, Marquis. *Andrew Jackson*. New York, 1933.

Jenkinson, Isaac. *Aaron Burr*. Richmond, Va., 1902.

Knapp, Samuel L. *The Life of Aaron Burr*. New York, 1935.

Lodge, Henry Cabot. *Alexander Hamilton*. Boston, 1899.

McCaleb, Walter F. *The Aaron Burr Conspiracy*. New York, 1903.

Myers, Gustavus. *The History of Tammany Hall*. New York, 1917.

Parmet, Herbert S., and Hecht, Marie B. *Aaron Burr*. New York, 1967.

Parton, James. *The Life and Times of Aaron Burr*. New York, 1858.

Robertson, David. *Reports on the Trials of Aaron Burr*. Richmond, Va., 1808.

Safford, William H. *The Life of Harman Blennerhassett*. Cincinnati, 1859.

——, ed. *The Blennerhassett Papers*. Cincinnati, 1891.

Sellers, Charles C. *Benedict Arnold*. New York, 1930.

Sparks, Jared. *Correspondence of the American Revolution*. Boston, 1853. 4 vols.

Todd, Charles Burr. *The True Aaron Burr*. New York, 1902.

Van Doren, Mark. *Correspondence of Aaron Burr and His Daughter*. New York, 1929.

Wandell, Samuel H., and Minnigerode, Meade. *Aaron Burr.* New York, 1927. 2 vols.

A Note to the Reader

If you have enjoyed this book enough to leave a review on **Amazon** and **Goodreads**, then we would be truly grateful.

The Estate of Noel B. Gerson

Sapere Books is an exciting new publisher of brilliant fiction and popular history.

To find out more about our latest releases and our monthly bargain books visit our website: **saperebooks.com**

Made in the USA
Columbia, SC
29 July 2021

42642921R00171